P9-CPY-366

Divorce Mediation

DIVORCE ✗ MEDIATION

How to Cut the Cost and Stress of Divorce

DIANE NEUMANN

HENRY HOLT AND COMPANY / NEW YORK

Copyright © 1989 by Diane Neumann
All rights reserved, including the right to reproduce
this book or portions thereof in any form.
Published by Henry Holt and Company, Inc.,
115 West 18th Street, New York, New York 10011.
Published in Canada by Fitzhenry & Whiteside Limited,
195 Allstate Parkway, Markham, Ontario L3R 4T8.

Library of Congress Cataloging-in-Publication Data
Neumann, Diane.
Divorce mediation: how to cut the cost & stress of divorce
Diane Neumann. —1st ed.
p.   cm.
Includes index.
ISBN 0-8050-0879-9
1. Divorce mediation—United States.   I. Title.
HQ834.N48   1989
306.8′9—dc19   88-28170
                                                    CIP

Henry Holt books are available at special discounts
for bulk purchases for sales promotions, premiums,
fund-raising, or educational use. Special editions
or book excerpts can also be created to specification.

For details, contact:

Special Sales Director
Henry Holt and Company, Inc.
115 West 18th Street
New York, New York 10011

First Edition

Designed by Katy Riegel
Printed in the United States of America
1   3   5   7   9   10   8   6   4   2

To Shel, for her invaluable support

CONTENTS

Contents

ACKNOWLEDGMENTS

I want to begin with a profound and heartfelt thank-you to Shelly Cullen. Her encouragement and enthusiasm never compromised her honesty as she reviewed my work, and I often recall her wry comment to me upon reading one of my early chapter rough drafts, "If you can write a book, I can do anything!" In addition, her assistance to my children was instrumental in allowing me to pursue this writing.

I want to thank my children, Brian and Stacey, who were considerate of the long hours I spent at the word processor. They were always ready to help out, and, indeed, we spent one vacation weekend brainstorming possible book titles.

My Peer Mediation Group devoted monthly meeting time to working on sections of the book, and I appreciate the generous contributions of Barbara Younger, Phil Woodbury, Stephen Shapse, Janet Wiseman, and especially Ron Fox.

My appreciation to my friends who supported me in every possible way: Ardath Garfield, Mary Tervo, Sandy

Acknowledgments

White, Linda Watkins, Sharon Jeffries, Kyle Slayback, Joan Chaput, Susan Getman, and Sally Bubier.

Thanks to my parents, Nancy and Paul Patania, and my deep gratitude to my cousin Carol, who provided the foundation for me to write this book.

I want to thank Marianne Takas, an author and friend, who showed me that it could be done—by writing a great book herself—and to my editor, Channa Taub, for helping me clarify my ideas.

A special note of thanks to the separating and divorcing men and women who, over the past seven years, came to me with questions about mediation. Before and after lectures, by telephone and letters, these questions, and the lack of another book that addressed their concerns, gave purpose for this book and outlined its structure.

Divorce Mediation

INTRODUCTION

Divorce mediation is one of the new catchphrases of the 1980s. Yet few people understand exactly how it works. This book will explain what divorce mediation is, why it is so successful, and how it can work for you.

Every year in the United States, there is one divorce for every two marriages. There will be 1.2 million divorces and 1.8 million separations this year. Each of you has already been affected by a divorce, whether it is your own, a family member's, a friend's, or a coworker's.

For those of you about to start your divorce procedure, this may be your first experience with a court system. Chances are it will not rate with the great firsts of your life. A divorcing couple enters a different and harsher world. Many people have described the adversarial system as notoriously expensive and more emotionally painful than the end of their marriage. Invariably they have found that litigation created added bitterness and acrimony. Divorce mediation was born to help alleviate this nightmare.

Mediation offers a commonsense way to settle a dispute. A neutral professional sits down with the divorcing couple and helps them reach a settlement. To date, only 3 percent of the divorcing population has used mediation, but experts predict that within the next ten years mediation will be the way most people settle their divorce disagreements. Why has it worked? Why does it offer such hope?

One of my favorite analogies may help to explain why mediation will be so successful. Take a barrel of money and place it between a divorcing couple. The adversarial system provides the divorcing couple one important rule: "Grab as much money from the barrel as you can get for yourself." What happens is certainly predictable: they each attempt to take all the money. Now let's put it into a mediation context. Here is the same barrel, placed between the same divorcing couple, with a very different rule: "How can you most fairly divide this barrel of money between the two of you?" Experience shows us that people will try to work out a fair settlement. The definition of *fair* is by far their biggest problem and the main reason for employing a professional mediator.

The successes of divorce mediation have convinced legislators and court officials to encourage and implement mediation programs. Currently ten states have mandatory mediation for divorcing couples, five states allow a judge to order mediation, and twenty-one states are considering mediation programs. Mediation is here, and with it comes a multitude of questions.

If you are like most Americans, you have barely heard the word *mediation*. Even divorce professionals aren't always certain what divorce mediation is all about.

Mediation started in the early 1970s with a nonprofit community program called The Bridge, in Atlanta, Georgia, which used mediation to bring together runaway children and their parents. The techniques and procedure were successfully transferred to divorce mediation, and it spread

like wildfire throughout the United States. It has come
the heels of no-fault divorce, which changed the way we
end marriages in the Western world. It eliminated the idea
of one person having to be the "bad guy" during a marriage.
Regardless of fault and regardless of the kind of divorce
filed, settlements are basically an economic matter of property division and support. Divorcing men and women are
beginning to realize that hiring top lawyers to wage their
battle is a sure way of escalating their divorce costs and
doesn't do as much for a fair settlement as reasonable negotiations would.

Divorce has become big business in America. Even low
estimates show that Americans spend at least two billion
dollars on divorce each year. Many researchers provide a
figure that is double this amount. Literally hundreds of
divorced men and women have confided to me that they
wish they had heard about mediation before spending $20,000
to $40,000 for a divorce court battle.

Along with lower costs, there are other good reasons for
using divorce mediation. Many people want a civil relationship after their marriage ends, and mediation minimizes
the bitterness. Recent clients of mine turned to mediation
for this very reason. Jack and Mary had been married twenty-
three years. Their oldest child was graduating from college
in five months and they both wanted to attend his graduation. Jack and Mary had just begun their divorce procedure and their relationship was rapidly deteriorating. They
decided to stop their lawyers from pursuing a contested
divorce and to try mediation. Both wanted a civilized relationship that would allow them to be in the same room
for future events involving their children. They simply wanted
a fair and decent divorce. Mediation helped them to achieve
just that.

1

What Is Divorce Mediation?

In eighteenth-century England, there was a custom called "jumping the broom." A woman and a man who wished to marry had to jump over a broom, taking care that no piece of their clothing touched the broom. If the woman's clothes touched the broom, it meant that she was pregnant or had lost her virginity. If the man's clothes touched the broom, it meant that he would prove unfaithful. Historians today describe this event as one of that century's common-law marriage rites.

Many of our laws are based on the old common laws of England; some of our divorce laws seem to make about as much sense as jumping the broom. Our present court system creates an adversarial contest between spouses seeking a divorce. Adversarial means "one who opposes or fights against another." We see the result when one divorcing spouse wins and the other loses. In all probability, the loser will then take the winner back to court again and again. All family members suffer emotionally and financially each time this occurs.

Divorce mediation is being heralded as a civilized way

to reach a divorce settlement. It can be used to reach one or more agreements, or to establish the complete divorce settlement. The method involves using a professional, neutral mediator. "Neutral" does not mean that the mediator has no feelings or opinions; rather it means the mediator does not actively take the side of either spouse. The mediator guides the divorcing couple using a structured, step-by-step approach. It is essential, however, that both spouses agree to mediation. It can't work with only one spouse wanting to use it.

During most of the mediation sessions, the clients and the mediator meet together. At times, the mediator may meet with the husband or wife separately; this is called "caucusing." If the mediator has a caucus with one spouse, then the mediator will also caucus with the other spouse.

Each mediation is tailor-made for the individual couple, but here are some of the areas that are typically resolved in mediation:

- Parenting arrangements for minor children. The courts call these arrangements "custody" and "visitation." They include present and future parenting guidelines, schedules, and changes.
- All the aspects of child support and future college expenses.
- The division of marital property, which might include a house, furniture, stocks, savings accounts, IRAs, pension plans, cars, and grown-up toys such as stereos and VCRs.
- Alimony—always a hot issue.
- Other assets, pension plans, and vacation and rental property may be addressed, as well as such sophisticated plans as stock options and tax shelters.

- All of the couple's debt is considered: charge cards, car loans, mortgages, personal loans, and even gambling debts. Divorcing people have a higher rate of debt than the average American; no one has quite figured out why.
- Medical and dental expenses and insurance, life insurance, and disability insurance. (This area ties into the support issues.)
- Self-employment income, which can present quite a challenge to people during divorce negotiations. All income must be verified, and self-employment income is not as easy to verify as employment income. However, this area is much easier to settle in mediation than in a contested courtroom battle.
- Business valuations and welfare regulations are some unusual areas that may play a role in working out a settlement.

Separating men and women are often shocked to discover that a judge has the final say over their divorce settlement. I have met many people who assume they can make any kind of a divorce agreement they want to, because "this is a free country." It may be a free country, but you cannot make any kind of divorce settlement you want. A state court must approve your settlement. This is an important function of a mediator—to frame a divorce settlement that the court will approve. At your final mediation session, you will be presented with a written Memorandum of Understanding. When both parties sign this document, it is a legally binding contract. This document is then submitted to the judge for approval, and becomes part of the divorce decree.

Mediation has been called a form of therapy. It isn't. It may be therapeutic, in the same way that the color blue is more soothing than the color red, but it isn't therapy. Mediation can be therapeutic because it:

- Creates a cooperative atmosphere.
- Clarifies the issues between spouses.
- Fosters clear communication between spouses.
- Keeps emotional tensions separate from financial decisions.
- Provides a neutral person to help both parties.

Mediation is therapeutic in that the process helps each person to heal emotionally by providing a means to work out the end of their relationship in a way that makes sense and is sensitive to their needs.

Couples often find mediation helpful because they need to know about divorce *before* the actual filing. There are millions of divorced people who become divorce experts after their divorce becomes final, when it is too late to use their knowledge. During mediation you'll acquire a lot of vital information, including:

- The latest divorce-related parenting information.
- Typical divorce settlement provisions.
- Specific financial tools.
- Methods for anticipating your future needs.
- The court's attitude toward similar divorce settlements.

All this information helps divorcing people achieve a mutually satisfying settlement that each person feels is fair and that both can live with.

How Mediation Proceeds

By now you may be wondering how an actual mediation works. Let's briefly take a look at the mediation sessions her clients of mine, Ellen and David, who have given .... permission for this outline. Ellen and David are a fairly typical couple, and though their specific sessions may differ somewhat from yours, there will be more similarities than differences. The following account is an overview; the actual dynamics and details of their sessions will be fully presented in chapter 4.

The First Contact

Ellen called me at the end of July with questions concerning mediation. She had heard of the method through a friend of hers and had read a newspaper article on the topic. She asked me the most popular question I get on that first call, "How long does it take?" The answer I give to everyone who calls is that the average mediation consists of five one-and-a-half-hour sessions.

One of Ellen's concerns was how to get her husband to come to mediation. As a first step, I offered to send a mediation packet to her. It was helpful for Ellen to have written material to show David, since he tended not to be responsive to any ideas from his soon-to-be ex-wife. (I would never just send out the divorce mediation packet to David, as he had not requested it.) He looked it over and decided to come to the introductory meeting with Ellen.

The Introductory Meeting

Ellen and David walked in to their initial appointment looking wary and anxious. I could almost hear Dave thinking, "What the hell am I doing here?" I began the meeting with a short description of mediation, since most people need such information—I have stopped being surprised at the number of people who are uncertain what they're doing in my office.

The first half of the meeting ended with an explanation of the guidelines of our sessions. There are three fairly simple rules:

1. Husband and wife will take turns talking.
2. Each will make a full financial disclosure of all income, assets, and liabilities (joint and individual).
3. Both will sign a mediation contract with me before we begin. It is a short contract that the three of us sign. This is the only document they sign during mediation.

During the second part of the meeting I gathered information about their specific circumstances: children, employment, finances, property, debt, insurances, temporary agreements, and other pertinent information. I looked for the kind of background material and financial information that I would need to mediate. Some of my questions were personal, such as, "Why are you getting a divorce?" and "Is there any way in which either of you could change that would make you want to stay married?" This type of information is necessary to successfully mediate a divorce. The emotional components in a divorce often play a key role in the negotiations. Understanding the emotional dynamics lets the mediator guide the couple out of any impasse.

This appointment also offered Ellen and David the chance to see if each of them felt they could work with me. Often people don't appreciate the value of personality compatibility. You should have the feeling that the mediator is competent and someone you'd like to work with. If you don't feel this way, it might be a good idea to interview another mediator. (This advice holds true for virtually every professional you'll ever have to deal with.)

By the end of the meeting, they wanted to start mediation, which, I pointed out, was their first agreement. They were each given a copy of the Divorce Mediation Contract (see Appendix I), and we made an appointment for the following week.

The First Session

Since this couple had children, we began our session with a discussion of parenting issues concerning Jennifer, age fifteen, and Jeff, age eleven. I explained the area of legal custody, which must be decided for all minor children. There are different types of legal custody, depending on which state you live in. Most individuals who mediate their divorce choose joint legal custody, though some choose sole legal custody. Joint custody, also called shared custody, occurs when both parents legally retain the prerogatives of being a parent; either may sign the medical permission form in an emergency room and either may sign their child's report card. (It doesn't mean both have to sign the permission form or the report card.) Sole custody, on the other hand, means only one person (the parent with custody) can sign the medical form or the report card. Ellen and David chose joint legal custody of their children.

Our next issue concerned the physical custody of Jennifer and Jeff—determining which parent the children will primarily live with. Most parents in mediation choose physical custody with one parent, though I am seeing more parents who choose joint physical custody. (Joint physical custody, in which the children live with each parent roughly one-half of the time, is talked about more often than it is done.) Not everybody is able to resolve the question of physical custody in one session, but David and Ellen had a fairly easy time making this decision; they both wanted Jennifer and Jeff to live primarily with Ellen.

The parenting schedule was our next step. (In the old days this was called visitation.) The entire area of parenting is probably the most important issue for families as it has far-reaching effects on the divorcing parents and their children, yet it receives little time or attention in the hands of most divorce lawyers and the courts. (Yet visitation is the single most common reason why divorced people go back to court.) In contrast to this approach, mediation stresses the importance of parenting guidelines and takes the time to work out a parenting schedule that suits the needs of both parents and children.

David had difficulties with Jennifer that seriously interfered with the parenting schedule, so we dealt with this immediately.

Like many of the people that I see during a first session, Ellen and David were not ready to make any permanent decisions at this time. Each person must feel totally comfortable with any and all decisions they make during their sessions. My purpose is to introduce and explain the area of divorce we are looking at, then to allow people time to consider the decisions they must reach. I am only too aware that for most people, this is the first time they have heard anything of what I am describing.

At the end of the first session I gave each of them a budget to complete at home.

The Second Session

The session began with my review of Ellen's and David's separate monthly budgets. Budgets are a useful tool to help focus on finances. The figures and the discussion gave me an idea of how much financial knowledge each person had. There is often an obvious imbalance in this area, and I must balance their knowledge of financial matters. In this case, Ellen did not have as much tax knowledge as David did, and I worked to help her gain the understanding she would need. (The mediator can either explain the information to the person who needs it, or refer her or him to another professional.) At the same time, I enlisted the support and cooperation of the more knowledgeable spouse—in this case, David; I helped him to realize it was in his best interest to have Ellen understand the decisions they must make together. Ellen was a fairly quick learner, though it wasn't an area she felt comfortable with. I find that nearly everyone can understand the basics well enough to learn what they need to know.

The purpose of this session was to discuss child support—a significant issue for parents. It is important to establish a support plan that both parents consider fair and that provides for the needs of their children. The definition of fair is more vital than most people realize. What matters in the long run, after the judge has approved the settlement and the lawyers have submitted their final bills, is that Ellen and David know that each got a fair deal. Otherwise, one or both may not live up to the agreement, may seek court action to change the agreement, or may personally strive to make their ex-spouse's life hell.

Several factors are taken into account in determining the amount of child support: each person's needs and expenses at this time and in the future, present and future income, a detailed examination of the state guidelines, and what each person considers to be fair.

The Third Session

The primary focus of this session was on the house. They had been in conflict during the entire time of their separation over the use of their house. Ellen wanted to remain in the house for several years with joint ownership, while David wanted the house sold now and the equity divided between him and Ellen.

A marital residence is often a hotly contested issue, with the most common disagreement focusing on whether to sell or to keep the residence, and who gets to live in it if they keep it. Their house was the main dispute between Ellen and David and the primary reason they wanted a mediator's help. We began looking at several options that were available to them but which they had not considered.

After the house discussion, I provided the necessary information concerning alimony. Alimony is often a loaded word for both men and women. Husbands tend not to want to pay alimony, and, nowadays, many wives are ambivalent about wanting to receive alimony. In the cases where the parties agree that support is required, though the payer (usually the husband) initially does not want to pay alimony, after understanding the tax implications, he often prefers to pay alimony rather than a maintenance form of support or a larger property division.

I ended the session by asking them to make a house contents division list.

The Fourth Session

The session began with guidelines for their continuing joint house ownership. Along with parenting disputes, joint ownership is a common reason people end up in court. It is important to make clear what each person's responsibilities are concerning the house.

We went on to review David's house contents list. Lawyers refer to this as the "pots and pans" issue. They often describe it as a volatile area that is difficult to settle. People who have gone to divorce court fighting over their house furnishings often spend thousands of dollars in legal fees to win items that are worth far less. An attitude of cooperation and mutual benefit goes a long way toward helping to work out who gets the pots and pans. The conflicts are easier to resolve in mediation. Ellen and David disagreed over three items, and as you will see in chapter 4, I was able to help them resolve this.

David's pension plan turned out to be a difficult issue to settle; the issue of pensions is often touchy. David initially felt that he was entitled to the entire pension, and Ellen seemed to agree with him. This is often a tricky situation for a mediator to deal with, since it feels to one person as if the mediator is taking sides. I explain to both individuals not only what I am doing, but why I am doing it—that correct and complete information is necessary if we are to create a settlement that lasts, one that is considered fair by both parties, and one that reduces the potential for litigation.

Like most of the people I see, neither David nor Ellen had information concerning marital property before coming to mediation. I explained the definition of marital asset: it is a very important term for people to understand, and it varies from state to state. Most states are equitable property states, while only eight states are community property states. This may not sound very significant, but it means that every asset you have, from your house to your pension, can be legally treated differently in each state. Equitable division means that the judge may assign property and assets to a spouse based on the judge's opinion about what is fair. Community property means that the spouses each own a 50 percent interest of the marital asset. You should understand the concept of marital assets in your state in order to make decisions concerning these assets. Once I describe the legal basis of pensions, there is frequently a lively interchange between the couple.

We continued with their remaining assets, and they disagreed over the division of their five-thousand-dollar bank account.

The session ended with a listing of joint debt and who would be responsible for the liabilities. Ellen and David were unusual in this often important area; they didn't have a large amount of debt.

The Fifth Session

This last working session dealt with some decisions they still needed to make: the division of their joint bank account and their house contents, and the payments of their children's college expenses.

The main areas of their divorce settlement had been decided, and this appointment focused on the details that had to be worked out. These details included future transfer dates for assets, their specific responsibilities for continuing joint ownership of their house, child support increases, and some minor issues.

They had almost completed the verification of all accounts by bringing in written bank statements, insurance documents, deeds to property, et cetera. They would send in any remaining documentation.

The Last Session

During the last session, Ellen and David reviewed the final written agreement, called "Memorandum of Understanding" (see appendix II). Each person received a copy of their settlement and a hearty congratulation for a job well done.

The entire mediation took them exactly two months; they filed for a no-fault, uncontested divorce in Middlesex County, Massachusetts, after our final session.

HOW DID
DIVORCE MEDIATION START?

In 1974, a man by the name of O. J. Coogler was on the board of directors of a nonprofit community agency in Georgia. This group was starting a new program called The Bridge, whose goal was to get runaway adolescents and their parents to sit down and work out their problems together. To achieve this difficult goal they decided to try a method called mediation. The program worked exceptionally well, better than anyone had dreamed possible.

The success of The Bridge set Coogler thinking. As a divorce lawyer and therapist, he experienced daily frustration with the emotional and financial problems faced by divorcing men and women. He asked himself if mediation could possibly succeed in another difficult context. Could this method be useful with a divorcing couple?

Coogler had been a lawyer for twenty years, then left his practice after becoming extremely dissatisfied with the adversarial method of divorce. In his book, *Structured Mediation in Divorce Settlement,* Coogler wrote that "in marital disputes, this legal struggle is frequently more damaging for the marriage partners and their children than everything else that preceded it." Eventually he changed professions and became a licensed therapist. Soon after the success of The Bridge program, Coogler created the procedure he called structured mediation in divorce settlement. Not surprisingly, he is considered the father of divorce mediation.

The procedure of mediation has a long history as an elite type of conflict resolution reserved for delicate international disagreements and complex labor-management impasses. You may have heard nightly news reports of international mediators scurrying between terrorists and powerful national leaders. Or you may have read about labor mediators meeting with General Motors' union and management leaders to ward off a massive strike. Until recently, however, no one had thought to use mediation to resolve a domestic conflict between two ordinary people. Coogler, however, saw mediation as a way to reduce the emotional trauma of the divorcing couple's struggle over their settlement.

In the amazingly short period of time since Coogler's idea was publicized, mediation has become the alternate way to reach a divorce settlement. Since 1980, divorce mediation is showing an astounding growth rate of 25 percent each year. Now it is being recognized as the civilized way to divorce in America.

Is Divorce Mediation Helpful Only for Custody Disputes?

A lot of people perceive divorce mediation as useful only in a contested custody battle. Divorce mediation first came of age as a way to resolve contested custody battles, and the method was immediately successful in reducing trauma and resolving the conflict. Now people are looking toward mediation to help in the financial areas of divorce settlement.

Mediation succeeded so quickly in the custody area because it answered a need that virtually every professional working with divorce knew was not being met. Professionals believed, and numerous research studies verified, that parents and children locked in a custody dispute paid a high emotional price for their battle. A prominent Massachusetts judge publicly stated that he'd rather make a decision on a death sentence than on a difficult custody case.

The following factors make custody mediation successful:

1. Both parents decide the parenting arrangements. Some sociologists have noted that Americans are not very good about obeying others when it comes to their children. A parent who didn't like a judge's decision simply appealed the decision in court or disobeyed it in practice. People often spent several years in court rehashing the same old fight.
2. Parenting arrangements are geared to the specific family needs, rather than following general rules that can't fit everyone's life-style. Mediation offers specific guidelines for divorced parenting as well as information on how similar situations were resolved.

3. Clients in mediation learn the skills necessary for resolving future disagreements about their children. There's
   probably no other skill that will be as helpful in their
   joint parenting. Situations change and people need to
   be able to change. Courts assumed people could negotiate their future parenting conflicts, but many people
   need to be taught these skills.

Over one-half of divorced people end up back in court
within one year of their divorce! The number one issue
they are fighting over is their children. Studies in Colorado
and California show that mediation reduces this litigation
rate. Mediated agreements last, and people don't constantly
drag each other back to court.

Why Has Financial Mediation Been So Long in Coming?

Three important reasons account for the late start of financial mediation. The first has to do with the background of
mediation; it was initially used by mental health professionals who were familiar with custody dynamics but had
little or no knowledge of the financial areas of divorce.

Soaring divorce costs are a second reason for the delay.
These costs are a severe problem for divorcing people, but
not necessarily for the professionals who earn an income
from them. Divorce lawyers are usually not happy about
turning over their income-producing clients to divorce mediators. The clients save money, but the lawyers lose a
lucrative source of income.

The third reason is that divorcing people have not had
the same exposure to financial mediation that they have
had to custody mediation. Much of the time people have

no choice with custody mediation—it is ordered by the court. Financial mediation is not yet court-mandated.

Though financial mediation may have been long in coming, it now offers a host of advantages over a court-fought divorce:

1. Mediation provides both husband and wife with a sound understanding of individual finances.
2. Mediation provides the opportunity for considering fresh options to help resolve financial problems.
3. It reduces conflict, thereby reducing the emotional trauma of financial disputes. This can benefit your children as well. Studies show us that children suffer whenever their parents fight. You might feel that if your courtroom battle with your spouse isn't directly about custody, it does not affect Johnny or Susie, but studies prove that children do indeed feel the pain of the battle, regardless of what issue you have chosen or been forced to fight over. Children often don't know what the fight is about; they only know that their parents are fighting.
4. The financial agreements, which include the important area of child support, last longer.
5. Divorcing people deserve a sane place to make their important long-term financial decisions. "Courtroom step" agreements (made by the couple's respective lawyers while literally on the courtroom steps) are not in anyone's best interest.
6. Mediation is an open process and allows for other professional input.
7. It saves each person the often excessive amounts of money that would be spent on litigation.

Financial mediation is, in fact, a type of mediation that we will see more and more of. Custody mediation has provided solutions in the very difficult area of custody disputes; now financial mediation will help the millions of people who are engaged not in custody battles, but in battles over money.

CAN YOU USE MEDIATION FOR ANY KIND OF A DIVORCE?

Very simply, yes.

Some readers may not be aware that there are two kinds of divorce in this country, fault and no-fault. A fault divorce means there are reasons, called grounds, for the divorce, and one spouse is legally to blame for the breakdown of the marriage. No-fault means both people believe the marriage is ending with no one legally to blame.

Divorce is controlled by state law, and each of our fifty states has its own set of divorce laws. The fault grounds for divorce differ from state to state, which creates severe confusion for divorcing people who move across state lines. Some of the more common types of fault grounds are adultery, desertion, mental or physical cruelty, chronic drunkenness, and insanity.

In 1970, the United States joined the rest of the progressive nations of the world when California introduced no-fault divorce. Since 1970, legislatures in every state in our country have passed no-fault laws. (When it was first proposed, many people were convinced the new law would lead to a dramatic increase in our divorce rates, but actually the opposite occurred.)

Lawyers using the adversarial process often use fault

grounds as a strategy. They may request a certain kind of divorce to enhance their client's precarious adversarial position or to scare the other spouse into agreeing to something else. The most typical example of this is when a parent counterfiles for custody of the children, claiming the other parent is unfit, because he or she wants to pay less money in support. Often the custodial parent is terrified of losing the children, and he or she will agree to less support rather than face a trial.

Most people filing for a divorce are not even clear about the kind of divorce they are getting. They may think they have filed for a no-fault divorce, when, in fact, the lawyer filed for a divorce on the grounds of mental cruelty. In fact, I've met hundreds of divorced men and women who don't know what kind of divorce they have received.

Another distinction plays a key role in divorce; a divorce may be contested or uncontested. Contested means that one of the spouses does not agree, either to the divorce itself or to the spouse's settlement offer. Uncontested means both people agree to the divorce and/or to the settlement. A divorcing couple and their lawyers who file for an uncontested divorce may have waged the most bitter, expensive, and vicious battle in their negotiations, but by the time they finally get to court, the disagreements have been ironed out and the divorce is filed as uncontested.

A contested divorce serves various purposes. It can delay a divorce if you don't want one, serve as a bargaining tool if your spouse doesn't want to be labeled as the one at fault, or show your resistance to the entire idea of a divorce. Years ago, preventing a divorce was a lot easier than it is today. Today you can slow the process down, or cause your spouse and yourself to spend a lot of time and money, but you cannot actually prevent the divorce.

To summarize, there are four types of divorce:

1. Uncontested no-fault divorce.
2. Uncontested fault divorce (with grounds).
3. Contested no-fault divorce.
4. Contested fault divorce (with grounds).

Most people who mediate their divorce settlement file for a no-fault, uncontested divorce. However, a small number of people do file for a fault divorce after mediating their settlement. Mediation can be used with a fault divorce or a no-fault divorce. It can be used to negotiate a settlement that was begun as contested. However, when the couple finishes mediation, their divorce (the settlement) is always uncontested.

Most people can use mediation, and they should consider mediation as a first step. Divorcing couples can always go to the adversary system if they don't like mediation. It is more difficult to go from the adversarial setting to mediation, and most people who do this are upset by the amount of money they have already spent on legal fees.

People who go from mediation to adversary divorce rarely feel that they have wasted their time or their money. Generally, the cost is minimal, and the men and women involved realize that their mediation was extremely helpful.

Some people assume mediation is only for perfect couples, meaning people who can communicate well and who are filing for a no-fault divorce. These individuals will certainly be able to use mediation, but it is the hostile couples who will benefit the most from this method. In certain situations, such as those involving people with mental disabilities, emotional dysfunction, retardation, or physically abusive relationships, mediation may not be appropriate.

Let me add that mediation is frequently used to resolve a single conflict. Mike and Joan came to see me concerning

Joan's moving out of state. They had been divorced for three years, and Joan wanted to take their two young children and move to South Carolina where her new husband was being transferred. Mike strongly objected and had spoken angrily of taking custody. Joan made threats of running away and spoke of wanting more child support. Four weeks later they had resolved their problem through mediation and came up with a plan that both felt was fair. Joan agreed to wait two years before moving, at which time Mike would be supportive of the move. They would share travel expenses for the children and change their parenting schedules to fit the new situation. Joan and Mike felt the scheduling changes were in the best interests of their children. I spoke with each of them shortly before Joan's move, and their situation was proceeding smoothly. Mike was behaving as he had promised, and everyone felt that the children and Mike would continue to be in close contact. Joan was making more money than she had been at the time of mediation, and they had worked out an arrangement whereby Joan would share the cost of sending the children by plane to spend time with their father.

Mediation may not work miracles, but you can use it in all kinds of divorces. The method can be started at any time during a separation or a divorce, and it can be used to resolve one conflict or to reach a complete settlement.

HOW LONG DOES IT TAKE?

Let me provide some background about the two phases involved in getting a divorce. The first phase is the settlement negotiations and the second is the routine filing for the divorce. You can, however, file for your divorce first, and then try to work out a settlement. The danger with filing first is that you may not have enough time to work out a settlement before your court date, and then a judge may end up making your decisions.

The filing is simply a request to a state court to approve your divorce and to schedule your day in court. The person who does the actual filing could be a paralegal, a clerk, a lawyer, or yourself, depending on which state you live in. If the court approves your divorce settlement, you are granted a divorce. Most states have a waiting period before the divorce is final.

Mediation is concerned with the negotiating phase of divorce. This is by far the most important and complex of the two phases. The mediation period generally takes six to twelve weeks. It takes more in the nature of six months to three years to arrive at a settlement with an adversarial divorce. Clearly there is quite a difference in the span of time required for an adversarial versus a mediated divorce. There are extreme examples, of course, and many of you probably know cases where the divorce has taken years to obtain. I hope none of you will compare to the man recently described in an article in the *American Bar Journal* who has spent the past twelve years actively pursuing his divorce. (In case you're curious, he still isn't divorced!)

There are several factors that influence how long it will take to reach a mediated divorce settlement. If the following factors apply, it will probably take longer than usual to work out your settlement:

- One person absolutely refuses to accept the end of the marriage.
- The couple has a complex financial portfolio that in-

25

cludes such investments as limited partnerships and tax shelters.

- One of the spouses is having an affair with the spouse's best friend.
- One spouse is self-employed, while the other spouse has absolutely no knowledge of the business.
- One person refuses to become informed about an important aspect of their divorce.
- Both are very silent and rarely take part in the mediation.
- Both spouses are extremely hostile and verbally attack each other.
- Both parents insist on full-time physical custody of their children for their own personal needs.
- The couple has been ordered to mediation by a court after an unsuccessful court trial.

People with the following characteristics will most likely have a shorter mediation:

- The couple chooses mediation voluntarily.
- Both have been emotionally healthy during their marriage and are in touch with how they feel.
- Each person can separate his or her anger from the concrete issues that must be resolved.
- Both can express angry feelings, rather than seeking revenge.
- Both want to make their own decisions.
- Each is willing to learn new information.
- Both are willing to let go of their marriage.
- Each has some respect for their spouse.
- Both are parents who want what is best for their children rather than what is best for themselves.

It is a couple's attitudes that determine how long they will take to negotiate their settlement. Reasonable men and women will most likely have a fairly short period of negotiations. In almost all cases, mediated agreements are more efficiently reached than adversarial agreements.

2

What Is Your Mediation Potential?

In spite of mediation's professional youth, some myths have already taken hold. One such myth is that you have to be having a friendly separation or divorce in order to use mediation. I have received numerous calls from professionals who say, "I have a divorcing couple who could benefit from mediation, but they don't get along well enough to use it." People fail to understand that mediation was specifically designed as a process to resolve disputes; it is expected that the parties are in conflict, or that they will soon have conflicting interests.

Even those who profess to know that mediation is appropriate for the vast majority of separating and divorcing people still maintain that if one or both clients express their anger loudly, the couple is not suited for mediation. Maybe because of my Sicilian background, I do not find this to be true. In fact, the most difficult couple that I worked with were two extraordinarily silent people. They consistently nodded, shrugged, or gave monosyllabic responses to my every attempt to elicit their settlement interests. The screamers were nowhere near as difficult as this couple was. It is not the verbal decibel level exhibited by clients that determines their appropriateness for mediation.

There are two primary factors that actually indicate a couple's appropriateness for mediation: the desire to avoid the adversarial arena and wanting a fair settlement. In my experience, most separating and divorcing couples are appropriate for mediation—some more than others. I have designed a questionnaire to help you determine your potential for mediation. Like all tests, it is not a foolproof guarantee of success or failure; rather, it provides a quick and easy method to help you determine your mediation potential.

The following questions should be answered by circling the response that applies most to your situation. Then add up the points and discover your potential for mediation.

Questions for all separating and/or divorcing couples:

	Yes	Maybe	No
1. Is your marital relationship over?	5	3	1
2. Would you prefer to spend the least amount of money necessary to reach a divorce settlement?	5	3	1
3. Would you prefer to spend the least amount of time necessary to reach a divorce settlement?	5	3	1

	Yes	Maybe	No
4. Can you be in the same room with your spouse for approximately one hour with a neutral third person present?	5	3	1
5. Do you believe your spouse will be honest about his or her income and assets?	5	3	1
6. Are you willing to work on budget forms (with needed help)?	5	3	1
7. Are you willing to do legwork, such as gathering your account and credit balances?	5	3	1
8. Do you believe your spouse will follow through with a fair agreement that he or she commits to?	5	3	1
9. Have you been truthful about money with your spouse?	5	3	1
10. Has your spouse been truthful about money with you?	5	3	1

	Yes	Maybe	No
11. Would you react negatively to legal techniques, such as a sheriff serving you with a summons?	5	3	1
12. Would your spouse react negatively to such an action?	5	3	1
13. Would you prefer not to pay large legal bills from joint assets?	5	3	1
14. Do you think you would obtain approximately the same settlement using mediation as you would using the adversarial approach?	5	3	1
15. Do you think you would receive or pay approximately the same amount of support using mediation as you would using the adversarial approach?	5	3	1
16. Would you prefer to have your negotiations handled in a private office rather than in a public courtroom?	5	3	1

	Yes	Maybe	No
17. Would you prefer not to be forced to testify during a divorce court trial?	5	3	1
18. Would you rather have all the necessary information before you reach a divorce settlement rather than after?	5	3	1
19. Would you rather meet with a neutral mediator than have two lawyers fight over your assets?	5	3	1
20. Are you considering or presently using mediation?	5	3	1
21. Will you follow through with a fair agreement that you commit to?	5	3	1

These responses are weighted significantly greater:

	Yes		No
22. Are you mentally competent?	5		− 100
23. Are you willing to be honest about your income and assets?	5		− 100

	Yes	Maybe	No
24. Are you physically abusive to your spouse?	−100		5
25. Is your spouse physically abusive to you or do you fear physical abuse from your spouse?	−100		5

Questions for separating and/or divorcing couples with children:

	Yes	Maybe	No
26. Would you say that your children's best interests are one of your priorities?	5	3	1
27. Would you prefer to make your own custody and visitation decisions concerning your children?	5	3	1
28. Are you willing to confidentially disclose any significant problems in your parenting?	5	3	1
29. Would you prefer that your children not be used as the prize of a custody battle?	5	3	1
30. Is it important to you that your children suffer from the divorce as little as possible?	5	3	1

Add up your total points:

Total points

120–150	Perfect for Mediation
90–120	Very Good for Mediation
50–90	Average Mediation Potential
30–50	Your Mediation May Take Longer Than Most
Below 30	Skip Mediation—Go Directly to Divorce Court

This score is not the only indication of your appropriateness for mediation, but you may regard it as a strong determinant of your potential success using divorce mediation.

3

Why Should You
Use Divorce Mediation?

There are three main problems connected with divorce today: the cost of working out the settlement, the failure of settlements to last, and the emotional trauma suffered along the way. The average divorcing couple has a little under $20,000 in net assets. Very few of these people want to spend a hefty chunk of their savings in an expensive legal battle to divide these assets. Men and women in the United States spend upwards of $2 billion per year obtaining their divorces. The constantly rising fees of divorce lawyers, expert witnesses, and other professionals have contributed to today's high costs. It's a problem people face for a long time after the divorce is final.

The cost of divorce holds every promise of continuing to climb. Ask any divorced person you know to give you a general idea of the cost of divorce. You will hear numbers that greatly surpass what you imagined a simple divorce could cost.

Mediation makes a significant difference in this area by reducing the expense of working out the settlement. Paying for two lawyers versus paying for one mediator is the first and most obvious savings. During an adversarial divorce, each party is paying their own lawyer to gather the information. Mediation uses only one professional, resulting in one-half the professional cost.

The second area of savings is in discovery motions. The legal system encourages lawyers to spend thousands of dollars requesting payroll deductions, payroll income, bank accounts, pension contributions, and a host of medical and disability plans. During mediation, each person simply brings in a copy of their wage stub, payroll deductions, and medical plans, thereby eliminating the expensive process of discovery motions.

The biggest savings, however, is achieved in the cooperative working out of the settlement. Rather than paying for two lawyers to work out the multitude of details in a divorce agreement, which then have to be checked with their respective clients, mediation allows the spouses to directly communicate with each other. This direct communication reduces the bulk of the money that most Americans spend on their divorce.

The savings obtained by using mediation increase in those cases where the divorce would otherwise be contested. It is not unusual for a contested divorce to cost $60,000 or $70,000. (Chapter 7 has more information about the specific costs of divorce.)

Kenneth Kressel, a famous divorce researcher, reports, "There is approximately a fifty-percent chance of a court contest in the postdivorce period." The reality of divorce is that, after spending thousands of dollars and hundreds of hours on reaching an adversarial settlement, these settlements are often broken. Nationwide, over one-half of divorced people are back in court within one year after their marriage has legally ended. There are many areas of disagreement that drive people back into divorce court, but the ones that are raised most frequently are the following:

- First and foremost are disagreements over parental visitation rights for the noncustodial parent (the parent who doesn't have physical custody).
- Nonpayment of child support is another reason many people return to court. National statistics show us that 54 percent of noncustodial parents do not pay court-ordered child support during the first year after their divorce. The percentage increases over the next five years to roughly 75 percent of parents not paying their child support.
- Fourteen percent of divorced people (mostly women) are awarded alimony or spousal support. Within two years of their divorce, over one-half of these women do not receive their support payments or get drastically reduced payments. Women who do not receive their payments must file a motion to go back to court to get their payments enforced. Enforcing payments is not as easy as one might expect.
- Forty-six percent of divorcing people own a house at the time of their divorce. Many of them end up with joint ownership after their divorce, and arguments over who will pay for repairs or improvements are common. Most divorce agreements do not describe who is responsible for house repairs and improvements, and too often these arguments wind up in court.
- A person bitter over the property division in their divorce will often file a suit simply to bring the ex-spouse back into court. (While speaking at a seminar this past year, I met a woman who had gone to trial over her divorce settlement. The judge had awarded her 40 per-

cent of the house equity [market value of the house minus debts on the house], while her husband received 60 percent of the house equity. She told me that even her husband's lawyer was surprised by the split. Still angry after all these years, she recently filed her newest complaint against her ex-husband over a minor matter. She readily admitted she's not really concerned with this minor issue, which was who should pay for their daughter's school trip, but that she is so bitter over what she sees as her unfair share of the house equity that she'll take him back to court on any matter.)

Mediation solves the problem of short-lived agreements by forging settlements that are followed. It accomplishes this in a host of ways, most importantly by involving both people in the decision making, and by considering and resolving potential problems before they arise.

The third main problem facing divorcing people today is the resulting emotional trauma of their getting caught up in the adversarial struggle. As one recently divorced individual put it, "The worst part of it was that we ended up really hating each other." Our divorce court system creates or increases the anger and distrustful feelings between divorcing spouses by encouraging a winner-take-all mentality. This is most destructive when clients are encouraged to fight a custody battle over their children. Parents who want to "win" the children from the other parent and force their spouse to "lose" their children face one of the most stressful and traumatic times of their lives. And so do their children.

The adversarial atmosphere leads to bitterness, which spills over into the negotiations and into future interactions between the ex-spouses. Pitting one spouse against the other in court is like pouring salt on wounds—it often finishes off any chance of the ex-spouses dealing reasonably with each other.

Many people want a civilized relationship with their ex-spouses. This is not true for everyone; some people assume that once the divorce is final, it's all right to be enemies. But people married ten, twenty, or thirty years frequently have a different outlook. After parenting children and spending a large part of their lives with each other, these men and women want to be able to attend a function together if they choose. They don't want to have to decide "Who gets to go to our son's wedding?" There are strong connections between ex-spouses. They aren't necessarily positive, but they are strong. They don't have to be turned into hatred toward each other.

Mediation makes a dramatic difference in helping you to maintain a civilized relationship. It's doubtful you'll end up with a Hollywood version of the perfect divorced couple, where you are each other's best friend. This is simply unrealistic for most people. But mediation can help to prevent the animosity we see and hear about from so many divorced people.

This past year I mediated the settlement of a couple who had one significant wish. Their daughter, who was living in a small town in Ohio, was expecting their first grandchild. My clients each wanted to be with her for the birth. Their daughter also wanted both of them to come. However, they assumed that as divorced people they would be too hostile toward each other to do this. They began mediation already angry, assuming that only one of them could fly out to Ohio to be with their daughter. Mediation helped them do what they wanted to do; they were both at the hospital when the baby was born. It was a boy.

WILL MEDIATION TAKE AWAY
YOUR ANGER?

A lot of people have a hard time dealing with the anger they feel during their divorce. Their spouse's anger is even harder to accept. Many people express the hope that mediation will "take the anger away." It won't necessarily stop your angry feelings, but it will help keep them from adversely affecting your major financial and parenting decisions.

People's concern with the damage that anger can do is legitimate. Too often the divorce process fans the fires of their anger or their spouse's anger, creating additional problems. All too often I hear this sort of story from a divorced person: "I'll never forget the day a sheriff pulled up to my house in a police car, actually came up to the house and served me with these damn papers. I was never so humiliated in my life. Imagine, a police car at my house!" After this kind of experience, the angered person is all too likely to seek revenge.

Anger expressed as a threat toward a spouse usually invites a vengeful response. One such scenario has the husband telling his wife, "If you make me angry, I'll never pay you a cent in child support." The threat is used as a way to control his wife. Sooner or later such a threat creates vengeful feelings in his ex-wife and she retaliates in some way.

Anger that spills over into the divorce negotiations is often the biggest problem facing lawyers, mediators, accountants, and judges. Divorce professionals privately tell the infamous Candlestick Story, about a couple who have finally finished their complicated divorce settlement when one spouse suddenly remembers they have not decided which one of them gets the candlestick they bought years ago during a trip to Mexico. A bitter disagreement begins. Their lawyers are helpless in the face of the argument. All the work that went into their settlement goes down the drain as each spouse adamantly refuses to accept a settlement that doesn't include the candlestick.

If a person's anger turns into bitterness, this feeling soon poisons all future contact between the two spouses. Take for example the case of a woman so bitter she wants to cut off all contact between her ex-spouse and their children; her bitterness takes priority over her children's needs for their father.

Mediation can help with the anger during this period in several specific ways. The process of mediation creates an open line of communication between the divorcing couple—and keeps the anger from closing what little communication exists between two people. The mediator may defuse the anger expressed between the couple by reframing a spouse's angry comments to the other and by clarifying what the spouse has actually said (and not what the person assumes he or she said). Statements can also be neutralized by the mediator taking the bitter thrust out of the verbal attack. Mediation takes the energy of anger and redirects it to problem solving. The mediator can separate the emotional anger from the financial areas of the settlement, so that the Candlestick Story need not occur.

Mental health professionals agree that angry feelings can actually be helpful during your divorce if they do not spill over into the settlement negotiations. Anger can have its positive side in helping one deal with the pain of divorce.

It's not easy to end a relationship. The attachment to a spouse may be so strong that you cannot leave unless you get angry. You may have to call up your anger toward your spouse to enable you to separate.

Or you may find anger easier to experience than sadness. Anger can be a protection against feeling the loss of your spouse. Many people have an easier time experiencing anger than sorrow. The sorrow may be put off for another day.

Anger can also help to dispel the depression that's often a part of the divorce process. This depression is a difficult stage to move out of, and anger may provide you with the energy to go ahead with your life.

Anger isn't always a terrible thing. Therapists agree it is emotionally healthier to experience your feelings than to deny them. Indeed, anger is one of the natural emotional stages of divorce and, in the long run, will help you move through the process of separating from your spouse. Mediation can help you to keep these often necessary but potentially dangerous feelings from spilling over into your divorce negotiations.

WHAT IF WE CAN'T COMMUNICATE?

Occasionally during professional gatherings I have had people say to me, "I was going to refer these clients to you, but they weren't the perfect couple for mediation." When I ask why, the response I get is something like "Oh, they don't communicate well enough with each other." It amazes me that professionals believe this is a prerequisite for mediation, since the clients are ending a relationship, not beginning one.

Mediation began as a way to resolve a conflict between two people; it evolved from a program that helped runaway adolescents and their parents talk to one another. These families were definitely not communicating; they could barely be in the same room together. Indeed, the purpose of mediation was to reduce conflict and allow them to talk to one another effectively.

People in the midst of divorce can rarely communicate effectively with their spouse. Since communication is important in reaching a settlement, the question is how to help people communicate. A good mediator helps divorcing people to do this in one of two ways, either by teaching them to talk directly to each other or by having them communicate through the mediator.

The first method, the direct approach, teaches people to talk directly to each other. This approach is the better one to use when mediating between individuals who will have considerable contact with each other in the future, as it provides people with the tools they need to talk to each other without the mediator. This is important unless you want to spend the rest of your days sitting in a mediator's office. Divorcing people with children will find this especially helpful in their future interactions as parents, since they will most likely have more contact with each other than they anticipated, or will ever want!

In the second method, the indirect approach, the mediator acts as an interpreter between the spouses. A mediator may choose this method for several reasons. I use the indirect approach if the spouses are just too angry with each other to be productive during a session, or if only one person is showing severe emotional stress. By using this approach, I take the sting out of someone's words and in a sense neutralize them for the other spouse to hear.

Clients may eventually learn the direct approach after several sessions using the interpreter approach. Most mediators integrate both methods into their practice. And on some days one approach works better than on others—

whether because of someone's mood, or a fight, or simply because of the topic of discussion.

Some people mistakenly think of mediation as a kind of couples' therapy that will bring them back together. Mediation offers therapeutic benefits, such as reducing trauma and stress and increasing communication, but it is not therapy. The spouse who believes that mediation may lead to reconciliation as well as the spouse who is fearful that mediation is a ploy on the other's part to bring them together, are both misunderstanding the goals of mediation. The role of communication in mediation is to expedite the resolution of specific issues and to facilitate the ending of the marriage. Mediation allows for reconciliation because it does not escalate the anger and destroy any chance of resuming the marriage. Mediation *allows* for reconciliation—it does not cause it.

Today's popular stereotype of the perfect couple is the couple who can communicate with each other. This is a rare model of behavior, even for happily married couples. Mediation allows for communication between people who seemed unable to do so, and it increases communication between those couples who have some ability or willingness to talk with each other. Communication, in this case, is not a path to reconciliation, though this can happen; it is instead a tool enabling the couple to make decisions that serve the interests of both.

WHAT ARE THE OTHER BENEFITS?

Over two million men and women are divorced each year. The couples who choose mediation do so for a variety of reasons. Many have problems and concerns that mediation addresses in a way that the adversarial arena cannot. Mediation offers several advantages in addition to the three main benefits we've already discussed.

- Mediation is fair to both people. This may come as a surprise, but many divorcing people want their settlement to be a fair one. Rarely does a day go by that a client doesn't say to me, "I want a divorce, but I want to be fair to her (or him)." An important benefit of fairness is the increased probability that the settlement will be complied with.
- The process creates a cooperative attitude rather than one of conflict. This problem-solving approach goes a long way toward explaining the success of mediation. Take the case of the two separating people who work together on their financial arrangements to minimize the amount of taxes they must pay to Uncle Sam. Now that's cooperation!
- Mediation allows men and women to make their own best decisions. They do not simply obey their lawyer's advice, regardless of the financial and emotional costs, no questions asked. Many competent and self-reliant adults live to regret the decisions that were made for them. It reminds me of the way things were twenty years ago, when people simply followed whatever the doctor ordered. During the past twenty years there has been a dramatic change in people's attitude toward medical care. Now patients routinely seek second opinions and often question their doctor before meekly submitting to the surgeon's knife. People need to bring this same self-reliance to the decisions they make in pursuing a divorce. Mediation is the place each person can make informed decisions.

- Mediation is a place to learn about the various technical aspects of divorce and to get the information you require. Clients who have been in mediation do not echo the all-too-familiar refrain of divorced veterans of the court system, "If only I had known that before my divorce."

  People who are pursuing divorce settlements can never have too much information. During my years with the federal Internal Revenue Service I met many people who suffered from not being given enough information regarding areas of their divorce settlement. In too many cases, a divorced woman would receive an IRS notice of taxes due on her alimony payments. She didn't know the payments were considered taxable income to her and required her filing quarterly tax returns. Now she had penalties and interest to pay on top of her additional income tax. It was information she would have been better off having at the time of her divorce—it would have saved her a lot of money.

- Another benefit is discovering and examining the available options for your settlement. People walk into my office assuming there are only one—at most two—settlement choices. In fact, there are usually several options. Helping to brainstorm alternative choices is one of the strengths of a mediator and one reason why settlements can meet many of the goals of both persons.

  Pension plans are a good example. Many people, both men and women, assume that whoever earned the pension should receive 100 percent of the retirement benefit. They don't know that in most states, pensions are considered a marital asset. This means that the pension is owned by both people, not simply by the person whose name the pension is in. There are many choices in the area of pension division, and mediation allows each person to examine the different ways of achieving an equitable division of a pension earned while married.

- Mediation allows you to hear both sides of the issue. This is quite different from a courtroom trial, where typically neither person knows what the other side will present in court. Often the first time they hear the other side of the courtroom drama, they don't even recognize it as what really happened and are shocked by the judge's ruling against them. Mediation, in contrast, helps you to hear the other side of an issue in a way that promotes a fair resolution.

- Mediated sessions open up the lines of communication between two people. Since a lack of communication is the major reason cited for divorce in the 1980s, most couples need a third party to help them communicate. In order to work out a good settlement, you need to be able to clearly express your real concerns and to hear your spouse's concerns.

- A major advantage of mediation is that it promotes the best interests of your children. This is a priority clearly not shared by the adversary system. A courtroom judge essentially chooses the interests of one parent over the interests of the other parent. Though both parents may be represented by a lawyer, children in a custody dispute rarely have their own lawyer. Yet many parents want to do what is best for their children. These individuals find that mediation offers a place to reach sound agreements concerning their children. (This issue is explored in more detail in chapter 10.)

- The average mediated settlement takes approximately two months. The average adversarial divorce (using lawyers to negotiate but not including a trial) takes almost one year. There is a tremendous pressure on you during the period of time the divorce takes. The longer the negotiations drag on, the longer you experience this stress and, of course, the more money you spend. Mediation is geared to the time frame of the divorcing couple and moves along according to their schedule, which tends to be a shorter time than the delay-prone adversarial process.

- The separation of emotions from financial decision making is a significant part of mediation. Everyone has feelings, but in mediation these feelings do not form the basis for making financial decisions. Allowing feelings to affect settlements can be dangerous. Take, for example, the spouse who desperately wants out of the marriage. That person will often agree to anything to get the divorce, but soon changes his or her mind and the ex-spouses end up in court. Similarly problematic is a spouse with uncontrolled anger. If the anger is allowed to spill over into the negotiations, it can cause enormous expense and trauma for the entire family, as well as lead to repeated courtroom trials. Divorce decisions are often important long-term financial decisions that shouldn't be based solely on an overwhelming emotional base.

- Mediation avoids the public display of private issues. Unless you have firsthand knowledge of the mudslinging that can take place during a messy divorce trial, you may not recognize how important a benefit this can be. Indeed, clients do get angry and call each other names in my office, but my office is a far cry from a public courtroom witness stand. Maintaining your dignity is important during divorce, when your self-esteem may already be low.

- Mediation empowers each person. The mediation process alows each person to take charge of their own life. This taking charge is the basic formula for being able to successfully get on with your life.

WHAT ARE THE RISKS?

Many of the things that we want in life involve an element of risk. Even if we try to play it safe, we are apt to find ourselves in the very place where most accidents occur—our home bathtub!

Divorce itself has an element of risk. Studies have shown that among the forty-two most stressful life events, divorce rates as the number two stressor. (Heading the list is the death of a loved one, though some would argue that divorce is more stressful than death.) Indeed, accident and illness rates are much higher for men and women who are in the process of divorce or recently divorced than for the rest of the population.

Though mediation reduces the dangers of an adversarial divorce, it is not without possible risks. Be cautious of these:

- Hiring an unskilled mediator is a risky proposition. Unfortunately every profession has its share of practitioners who are not skilled at what they do. Since mediation is not an old practice, the small number of current mediators are highly skilled individuals establishing a new profession. But as this field increases, it will most likely have the same problems as other professions in guaranteeing the quality of its practitioners. Your mediator is not well skilled if he or she:

1. Acts solely as a referee for the divorcing couple.
2. Makes decisions for you.
3. Always takes the side of one person against the other.
4. Is not knowledgeable about state divorce laws, federal taxes, pension rules, etc. The mediator does not need to know everything concerning these areas (no one professional is an expert in every area), but the mediator should know when such information is necessary and how to get it.
5. Has a bias that affects every decision.
6. Makes a financial contingency fee arrangement with you. Contingency means that the price for the mediation depends on the settlement itself, such as 25 percent of any support paid. Mediation fees should be based on an hourly rate.

- A mediator who is not sensitive to power imbalances in the relationship of the divorcing couple will be ineffective at best and most likely destructive to the goal of a fair settlement. Some mediators don't understand the dynamics of power relationships and may simply act as bystanders, allowing the stronger spouse to get more than what is fair. For example, take a situation where the husband has a well-paying job, extensive financial knowledge, and makes all the family's financial decisions. The wife, in this case, has never worked outside the home, has no access to the checkbook, and must ask her husband for money. The mediator has to be concerned with balancing their financial expertise by providing the wife with the information she needs to make informed decisions.
- A definite risk exists if your spouse is dishonest about money with you. Some people think a spouse who is honest about having an affair will also be honest about

money. That's not necessarily true. You are probably the best judge of your spouse's financial honesty. If you have any doubts in this area, don't use mediation.

There is a related question that I am frequently asked. "What if my spouse has money hidden in an unnumbered Swiss bank account? Will it come out in mediation?" If a hidden asset is a concern of yours, such an asset will not be revealed during the sessions unless you or your spouse mentions it. However, it will not be routinely discovered during the adversary process either. Lawyers do not routinely track down unnumbered Swiss bank accounts. If you are worried that your spouse has any hidden assets, you are not a good candidate for mediation.

- If your spouse is actually involved in criminal financial dealings, be wary of using mediation. Any involvement with fraud, embezzlement, or other criminal activity requires legal help. Get yourself to a good lawyer specializing in criminal law. Your divorce settlement will not be easy.

- If you or your spouse is mentally incompetent, mediation should be undertaken only with special arrangements. One option is to have a close, responsible person take an active part in the mediation. This person can be a parent, sibling, or friend who must be present during every session. You may want to add the services of a lawyer and a therapist in this difficult situation. Mediation is flexible enough to allow for special situations, but this really depends on the willingness and skills of the mediator.

- If there is current physical abuse, I don't believe that mediation is appropriate. There is a range of opinions concerning mediating domestic violence cases. Many private mediators do not think mediation can work when physical abuse is involved. However, many court personnel routinely use it in this type of situation. Since most domestic violence cases end up within the court system rather than with private mediators, this is probably a public policy issue rather than an issue for private mediators to determine.

- If the mediator has a prior relationship with either spouse, it is best to refer to another mediator, as many professionals think that any kind of prior relationship has a potential for creating a problem. If the mediator does have a prior relationship with one spouse, be sure to discuss the possible consequences. You need to consider what effect this will have and what other options are available.

If you know the risks of mediation, you can work to avoid or minimize them.

4

A Mediation Case Study

There are some people who assume that mediation means compromise. It doesn't. Mediation can make it possible for each person to get what he or she wants.

The following is a mediation case study. It describes the actual sessions of Ellen and David Robertson, who came to me for divorce mediation. Each gave permission for me to tell their story. Their names and some of the details of their lives have been changed. The complete Memorandum of Understanding of their settlement appears in appendix II.

Introductory Meeting

The first time David and Ellen walked into my office I was struck by their icy politeness. David was tall and thin, with slightly graying hair. He wore a conservative blue suit and held himself rigidly, even while he walked. He sat down in my office and stared straight ahead at the wall behind my head.

Ellen's appearance was in direct contrast to her husband's tailored look. Her long dark hair was mussed; her casual, bright clothes hung loosely on her body and seemed at odds with David's somber suit. The most riveting feature about her was the piercing glare she cast at David.

After our greeting, I described mediation and how it was used to reach a divorce settlement and responded to their questions and concerns. David asked questions but rarely made eye contact with Ellen or with me as he spoke. Ellen continued to glare at David and did not ask any questions.

During the second portion of the session I took down their marital history and other necessary information. Ellen seemed eager to answer my questions, while David recited his answers briefly. Ellen and David had been married for nineteen years. They had not been getting along for quite a while, and David had first talked of getting a divorce six months ago. They began couples counseling; one month later he moved out of the house and was openly seeing another woman. Now only Ellen was seeing a therapist. Ellen was very angry and shocked over his leaving. Their two children—Jennifer, age fifteen, and Jeff, age eleven— were living with Ellen. Both Ellen and David described Jennifer as very angry with David.

The financial picture of this couple was typical of many middle-class suburban families. David, at age forty-one, was a regional manager for a high-tech firm and earned $51,000 last year. Ellen worked part-time as a library assistant and earned $1,900 during the year. They owned a single-family house, two cars, and seven rooms of furniture and had over $5,000 in their joint bank account. David had some stock through work—he wasn't sure how much—and he belonged to the credit union. He had a pension, and I told him we'd get more information on the pension at a later session.

I described what was considered marital property in this state. I reviewed their liabilities, which were fairly minimal and included their house mortgage, one car loan, and outstanding charge card balances totaling approximately $2,000.

Since their separation, David had continued to pay all of the house expenses: mortgage, utilities, insurances, and taxes. In addition, he was also giving Ellen $250 weekly for food and miscellaneous expenses. This money amounted to almost as much as the entire family lived on before the separation. David said, "I don't have any money left to live on." Ellen's response would not be described as sympathetic.

They had each been to see a lawyer for a divorce consultation, as each was concerned about their house. The house was their primary source of conflict, and they had been arguing over this since the day David moved out. Ellen was determined to continue living in the house until the children were through school. David wanted the house sold now.

I asked them why they wanted to use the mediation process to reach their divorce agreements.

Ellen replied, "My brother Bob and his wife just had a horrible divorce. His legal bills alone are $43,000 and they are still fighting. I heard that mediation would be a way to avoid that."

David spoke quietly, "Yes, we didn't want to spend everything we've saved over the years in order to get a divorce."

"He's just afraid I'll take him to the cleaners."

"I am not. I thought mediation would be fair, what's the matter with that? I thought we could give it a try. I know a lot of divorced people at work and they all tell real horror stories about what it was like to work out their settlement."

"Now you're going to try and take the credit for us coming to mediation? It was my idea, David, or did you forget that too?"

"I was the one who called the mediator."

I interrupted because by then I was getting a clear idea of their pattern of fighting, and the arguing was not productive. I explained the choices they had regarding their mediation sessions: they could be seen jointly or separately. In order to attend sessions together, however, each would have to make an effort to keep their comments under control. I reminded them that being seen together was more efficient, and less expensive. But if they each wanted to argue or make insulting comments, I recommended separate mediation sessions.

David looked at Ellen for the first time and said he thought they should attend the sessions together. Ellen nodded her head quickly. I told them that they had reached their first agreement quite easily.

I asked them each to tell me why they were getting a divorce. I explained that this information helps me to resolve the disputes and stalemates that come up during the sessions. Providing an explanation for why you want a divorce is not always easy, but David and Ellen, like most people who come to my office, found they wanted to tell their story.

Ellen looked away, apparently unwilling or unable to begin, so David spoke first. "I married when I was young. Ellen is a wonderful person and I love her, but I haven't been happy for a long time. We've tried to work it out, but I need to be living on my own."

Ellen had been watching David intently as he spoke. Suddenly she said, "We have not tried to work it out, not really. I still don't know what he wants. He's the one who wants the divorce. I know he hasn't been happy, but I haven't been happy either and I wanted to work on our problems. And now he's found someone else." She looked at him angrily. "So we're getting a divorce."

I asked Ellen if she thought that the marriage could continue. She said, "No, I know now that he's definitely leaving me. I know that it's over." I asked David if there was any way that Ellen or he could change in order to continue the marriage, and he said clearly, "No, there just isn't. It's too late." I ask these questions to be as certain as possible that both people acknowledge that the marriage is over.

At the end of the introductory meeting, they chose to go ahead and use the mediation process. The meeting ended with an outline of the topics we would discuss during each session. I also told them that they'd probably need five or six sessions to reach their final settlement. They were a fairly typical divorcing couple, with one spouse wanting out of the marriage and the other spouse angry with this decision but accepting the inevitability of it.

Next week we'd begin with the area of parenting, better known in the legal world of divorce as custody and visitation.

First Session

During this session, Ellen appeared more comfortable than she had the previous week. David, however, seemed nervous and still did not make eye contact with Ellen or me.

I outlined the three areas of parenting to be resolved: legal custody, physical custody, and a schedule of times spent with the children for the parent who isn't living with them. (If the parents choose joint physical custody, we work out a schedule for all family members.)

After hearing the information concerning legal custody, Ellen asked: "If we have joint legal custody, do we both have to sign every form our kids bring home from school?" I explained that in most situations this kind of custody works a lot the way things did during the marriage. If Jeff gets a detention and the school sends a note home for a parent to sign, either she or David could sign. If Jennifer needs to have her appendix out, only one parent has to sign the medical permission form. However, under joint legal custody, both parents would have to agree to any voluntary medical procedure—if, for example, Jennifer wanted to have her nose shortened or lengthened or simply changed in shape, at least while she is a minor (which in this state is under the age of eighteen).

Ellen asked, "What about the everyday decisions about Jen and Jeff? I don't want to have to call David about every little thing." I explained that in shared legal custody, the parent the children live with makes all of the day-to-day decisions, and that this is different from sole legal custody, in which one parent has legal custody and makes all of the decisions. David seemed to be listening very intently. Suddenly he said, "I don't want to be one of those fathers standing in the emergency room and not able to sign the form for one of my kids to get medical attention."

I said that David sounded as if he wanted shared legal custody, and he nodded. Then I turned to Ellen and asked which she wanted. She said, "I want the kids to know that he's still their father so I guess I want joint legal custody." David looked at me for the first time during this session but did not say anything. I asked him if he had something to say, and he replied, "I really wanted to share the legal custody and I've been worried that Ellen might not agree to it." I asked Ellen if she wanted to add anything. She said that she didn't. I reminded them that, according to the format of the mediation, each decision was always tentative, and they could always change their minds. I told them to think about every decision they make, and I encouraged them to bring up any concerns at the next appointment.

Their second parenting decision concerned who the children would live with. In legal language, this is called primary physical custody. Both parents wanted Jennifer and Jeff to stay together and to continue living with Ellen.

The main part of our discussion for the remainder of this appointment concerned David's time with each of the children. Since Ellen and David had already been separated for several months, I asked him to describe the time he spent with Jennifer and Jeff now. He tensed and replied very quietly: "It's not really going all that well."

Ellen added: "It's terrible. Jen is so mad at him she won't go with him at all. She told me she couldn't stand to be with him because he's seeing that woman." David seemed to shrink lower in his chair. Ellen continued, "When David found out that Jennifer wouldn't go, he didn't come by at all." Both parents apparently failed to consider that although Jennifer wouldn't see her father, Jeff might still want to see him.

We talked about the assumption that both children had to be together in order to spend time with their father. "I assumed they were all mad at me and that's the way it had to be," David said. I asked him if he wanted to see Jeff separately from Jen, and he said that he definitely wanted to be able to do that. I turned to Ellen and asked how she felt about the idea. Her voice softened. "I know that Jeff really misses being with his father. I'm glad if he can see him."

I helped them to interpret Jennifer's behavior by explaining that adolescents often express their anger toward a parent more than younger children do. All parents worry how their children will react, but rarely is a parent prepared for the anger and the moral indignation that adolescents and young adults may express. We talked about what is important for children of divorcing parents, and I provided some research material and information concerning children. I referred them to the book *Surviving the Breakup*, which has information for divorcing parents about their children, and to *The Kids' Book of Divorce*, an excellent compilation for parents and children that was written by children whose parents divorced.

We talked about a child's need for both parents. Soon David and Ellen began to set up a parenting plan based on this new information. After discussing several options, they wanted to try the following schedule: Jeff would spend every other weekend with David, from Saturday morning to late Sunday afternoon. David would also see him one evening during the week. David and Jeff would decide which evening this would be and inform Ellen at least one week in advance.

I encouraged them to create a specific plan for David to spend time with Jennifer. He said he would set aside one night a week to take her to dinner or a movie. I pointed out that she might not agree to it and that he might have to call her consistently and invite her to be with him. I asked Ellen what she thought she could do to be supportive of Jennifer being with her father. Ellen said that she would talk to her in a positive way about doing that. This was important because Jennifer might interpret her being with

David as somehow betraying her mother. Ellen became teary-eyed and I asked what was the matter. "I feel that I aggravated Jennifer's anger toward David. I was so damn upset that he left me. I mean, after all these years together. And I had only Jen to talk to—I didn't even want to tell my friends. I thought he'd change his mind."

I reassured Ellen that her feelings were understandable. I pointed out that she could be helpful to Jennifer now by explaining what she had just told us and by supporting her daughter's seeing her father.

We completed their parenting schedule: holidays, travel, vacations, religious upbringing, and special agreements. I congratulated them on completing a difficult session and they both seemed relieved to have it end. They each received budget sheets to complete for the next session. Right on cue, they both groaned!

Second Session

Ellen was clearly anxious when she walked into my office this session. David, on the other hand, seemed almost cheerful.

When I asked if there was anything they needed to bring up or ask before I began the session's topic, Ellen said: "I don't know if this is the right time for me to say this, but I hate it when he just walks in on me." David seemed stunned. "I have never just walked in on you. I'm only picking up the kids. What the hell do you want from me? Here, take the goddamn key." He took a key out of his pocket and angrily put it on the table. Ellen ignored it.

Conflict over a house key is a common problem for many separating people. Ellen continued, "When I told my lawyer about it, he advised me to change all the locks in the house." I looked to see David's response, and he was visibly furious. "How could you ever do that to me?" he asked.

Ellen didn't respond, and I asked her why she hadn't changed the locks as she had been advised to do. She replied, "I know David would be just too mad at me if I did. And I think it's a rotten thing to do. I couldn't hurt him the way he hurt me."

We talked about each of them needing and being entitled to privacy. David started to calm down, and I asked him how he would feel if Ellen had a key to his apartment and was able to come in. "It's not the same—I still own the house. But I get the point. I wouldn't want her to be able to walk into my apartment." Ellen quickly jumped on that remark. "You sure as hell wouldn't want me to walk in on you and *her*."

David ignored her comment, and I asked him why he wanted to keep the key if it wasn't to walk into the house. "I want to have a house key in case of an emergency with the kids and in case something happens to the house. After all, it's still my house." I asked Ellen how she felt about him having a key if he only used it for an emergency with the children or the property. "All I want is for him to knock first and wait to be invited in. The key isn't the issue. I never said that he couldn't have a key. He should have one in case something does happen. It's his just walking in the house that drives me crazy." David picked up the key. "I'll knock. You just weren't clear about it before."

The main topic of this session was support. David immediately began complaining. "I don't have any money and Ellen needs to get out there and work." As Ellen seemed about to verbally erupt, I defused the situation by explaining that we would discuss the subject of money using a structured approach. I began by reviewing out loud each of the budget forms they brought back with them. These forms provide information on the amount of money each needs to live. David had a more difficult time completing the expense portion of his budget than Ellen, as he hadn't gone through a winter in his apartment and had no idea what his heating bills would be. We came up with an estimate. Ellen figured out her expenses by going through the joint checkbook. Clothes and miscellaneous were the most difficult items for them to determine (as they are for virtually everybody), and I helped them to devise estimates in these two categories.

The second part of the session focused on income. David was continuing to pay all the bills after he left, though neither had any idea how much money this was. We determined he paid $1,025 a month for mortgage payments, real estate tax, house and car insurance, utilities, health insurance, and charge card payments. This was in addition to the $1,000 per month in cash that David was giving Ellen. Subtracting his apartment expenses from his paycheck, David was left with only $591 per month to pay all his other expenses, and he was quickly sinking into debt. I explained that this was a typical situation, as they now had two living quarters to support. Both were anxious during the budget review, but Ellen was quieter than usual. I asked her if she wanted to say something, and she responded, "I didn't realize that David had so little money for himself, even though he kept complaining. Everyone told me that men always complain. But I don't have much money either." I explained that they would have to divide up the money they had fairly, change their life-styles, or increase the amount of money that was available.

We continued with the income portion of the budget. Ellen's income was very low, as she worked only two afternoons a week at the local library for four dollars an hour. She had assumed she would go back to work, but now wasn't sure what to do because of the advice she had been given. She told us that several friends who had been divorced insisted that she would be better off if she had no income. The look on David's face clearly showed his anger at this comment. I asked Ellen how she felt about the advice she had received.

"I know that David can't just support me forever," Ellen responded. "He doesn't make enough money. But everyone, and I mean everyone, insists that I'd be better off not working." I asked Ellen to clarify what she meant by "better off." She said, "Well, that I'd get a lot more money from David in alimony."

David's silence was deafening, and I turned to him and asked him to comment. He spoke through gritted teeth. "I thought we were in mediation because we didn't want to play those games. I seem to be the only one not playing games in here." I pointed out to David that Ellen was only relaying what she'd been told by others.

I asked Ellen what she wanted to do about the need for more money. "I think that I can work more hours and make more money. I just didn't want David to get rich off of me." David looked at her in amazement. I explained that one purpose of the budgets was to provide a realistic view of their money situation and to clarify the financial circumstances of each party.

We talked about Ellen's potential employment and income. David said, "I know that she can make a lot more money." I turned to Ellen and asked her if she had any plan concerning this. She said that she knew of an available job for thirty hours a week working for a local newspaper at almost double what she made now. "We know the editor,

Mark Watkins," Ellen explained. "David never liked him because Mark seemed interested in me. But that won't stop me anymore." David just shook his head and let out a sigh.

We also looked at the child care situation in terms of Ellen's increasing her working hours: David and Ellen felt comfortable with the arrangements they could make for Jeff.

We went on to discuss child support. I had given them a copy of the state child support guidelines and calculated that the amount of child support David would pay if they followed the state's guidelines was $338. I outlined the factors that go into reaching a child support amount and encouraged them to address each one. David said that he would pay more than the suggested state guidelines until Ellen was earning more money, as long as she was looking for work. They agreed that David would pay $370 per week in support, and Ellen would pay all the household bills from that.

Another aspect of their child support discussion included the duration that child support would be paid. Ellen wanted child support until Jeff was out of college. David's legal obligation to pay child support ended at age eighteen, but he said that he would support the children if they were full-time college students. They agreed that support would continue until a child completed undergraduate school or reached age twenty-two, whichever occurred first.

I explained the tax consequences of child support. The payments were not taxable to Ellen on her federal and state returns as they are included in David's income. I pointed out that the IRS had ruled that the custodial parent, in this case Ellen, is entitled to a child exemption, and that that parent can give it to the noncustodial parent. I worked out the figures to help them understand the consequences of decisions in terms of money rather than tax theory and talk. I determined the filing status of each person, David's at 28 percent federal tax and 5 percent state tax, and Ellen at 15 percent and 5 percent respectively. That meant that a child exemption to David meant $560 and to Ellen it meant $300. Ellen would have Jeff as a tax exemption, and David would have Jennifer. They agreed on a 15 percent reduction in support when Jennifer reached "emancipation," and a reduction when Ellen earned over $25,000.

The next session would examine alimony and introduce marital property. I gave them some written information to review before the next meeting, and asked them to bring in a copy of their house deed, their mortgage balance, and some account balances.

Third Session

When Ellen and David walked in they casually commented about the weather, but it was obvious that they were tense. I suspected that one of today's topics—the house—might be the cause. There were still some decisions they needed to make concerning support. I asked if they wanted to finish support or start on the house.

Ellen answered at once, "I really want to decide once and for all what we are going to do with the house. But I also like the order we're going in, and I really think that we should finish the support part. We can't have that much left to do."

David nodded. "I would rather tie up one piece before we start on another."

We spent the first half of the session completing support. They had each received conflicting opinions from their attorneys on whether or not David would be required by a court to pay Ellen alimony. Alimony is often the most difficult area of divorce because there are few laws related to it and high emotions surrounding it. The tax implications of alimony are that it is deductible to David, which meant that he could subtract it from his gross income, and that Ellen was required to add the amount of alimony that she received from David to her taxable income, and to pay taxes on the money. I helped them to fill out forms so that they had a working knowledge of how the tax consequences actually affected each one of them.

Based on their tax situation, they decided to increase the support to $390 but to call $250 child support and $140 alimony. Alimony is deductible for the payer, so David benefited. To compensate Ellen for the tax she would have to pay on the alimony, he increased the figure by $20. Because of Ellen's lower tax bracket, they both came out ahead.

David said that he couldn't believe the difference that calling support alimony made to their incomes. These differences still apply but to a lesser extent, since the 1986 tax change has minimized the tax advantages of alimony.

The alimony payments end upon Ellen's remarriage or her death. Because of the first condition, it does not make sense for women who plan to remarry soon to accept alimony instead of child support. Ellen did not plan to remarry soon, and she wanted to receive support after the child support ended.

They agreed on alimony being a fixed amount with an annual cost-of-living adjustment, and that the amount of alimony would decrease when Ellen earned more than $25,000 per year (in 1988 dollars) and would end when she earned $35,000 per year (also in 1988 dollars).

David wanted to know, "What happens if I lose my job

or get laid off?" I told him that they could put in a provision to adjust the alimony because of an involuntary reduction in earnings if Ellen agreed to it. We discussed the implications of this clause, and Ellen said, "I don't have any problem with that."

During the second half of the session we began the house discussion. They began arguing with each other immediately.

Ellen stated, "The house is for the kids. That's why we bought it. He just walked out on me—why should he take the house from us?"

"You keep forgetting that you're the one who told me to leave," David replied. "It's my house too."

During their legal consultations, each had been told to expect a different result as to the division of their house. Ellen's lawyer had told her she would be entitled to live there until Jeff was eighteen. David's lawyer had told David that he would be able to get the house sold now if he needed a place to spend a lot of time with the children, the theory being that they could find two much smaller houses that each could afford. As Ellen heard what David had to say, her angry expression changed to one of fear: "Now you're going to try and get the kids. Just try—see how far you get!"

I intervened to clarify to Ellen that David was simply relaying what he had been told, in much the same way that she had relayed what her friends had told her regarding not working to obtain more support. I asked David if he was changing his mind about physical custody. "I'm not going to take the kids. I'm just telling you what was said to me."

I asked each of them to tell me what he or she wanted to do with the house. Ellen explained, "I want to live in the house because the kids have their friends there and go to school in the town and because, well, it's our home. He's the one who wants out. Why should we have to leave our home too?"

David, who seemed to be trying to stay calm, said, "I thought that we could sell the house so each of us has money to buy a condo. I just don't want to be paying rent for the rest of my life."

Ellen's voice rose quickly. "What are you talking about? We're not talking about the rest of your life!"

David responded, "What if you don't want to leave?" Ellen looked at him uncomprehendingly. I asked David if he wanted the house sold now, or if what he wanted was assurance that it would eventually be sold. "She can stay in the damn house now. I know that all of them want to live in it. It's their home. But this thing isn't easy on me either. No one seems to give a damn about me."

Ellen didn't respond right away, but there was a different look in her eyes. "I just want to stay in the house while the kids are in school, David. I don't want to live in that big house by myself once they're gone."

I presented several house options, including both selling their house and keeping it, and described the possibility of taking out an equity loan. Until this session, neither had thought it possible for divorcing people to take out a line of credit. (Often mediators wear a number of hats; banker and real estate broker bonnets are among the more popular.) We reviewed the advantages and disadvantages of this kind of loan and I suggested that each talk to a banker for further information if they were interested in pursuing this option.

The house discussion also included capital gains tax consequences, and Ellen said, "I'm actually getting the idea of taxes, though I still hate the whole subject."

They agreed to sell the house within one year of Jeff's

high school graduation or if Ellen remarried, or if she and David agreed to sell it sooner. We discussed exactly what would be subtracted from the sales price, and who had the first option to buy. I reassured them that they did not have to have their house appraised now, as they only needed a value if they were to divide it now or set the final price at this time. David glared at Ellen, and when I asked what this was about, Ellen explained, "My friends told me that I'd have to have the house appraised, so we had one done two months ago. And paid $275 for it." (This unnecessary expense illustrates why you should consult with a mediator before taking these kinds of actions.)

I asked them to consider during the time between mediation sessions the option that seemed to satisfy each of their goals. This plan was twofold: it called for Ellen to continue to live in the house until one year after Jeff graduated from high school and for Ellen to sign a line of credit with David so he could get some of his equity out of their house, with David responsible for the payments. We scheduled our appointment for the week after next, since David would be out of town until then.

Fourth Session

David and Ellen came to the session separately and greeted each other almost pleasantly. We returned to the discussion of the house almost at once. They expressed surprise that a solution had been reached that let each of them get what they wanted.

I focused on the details of their continuing to own the house jointly. They agreed to split the cost of some repairs, but disagreed as to which expenses they would split. I asked them to try to be specific about exactly how they wanted to pay for repairs to the house, from a broken window to a burst furnace. Ellen said, "I think we should both pay for all the repairs that the house needs."

David looked at me and countered, "But she's not realistic. What about a broken window? It doesn't make sense for us to have to sit down and discuss every little thing. I give her too much support now, that should be enough to cover those things." "What do you mean, 'too much support'?" I intervened then, and asked David how he wanted to handle the cost of repairs. He nodded, "I own the house as well, of course I should be responsible for major expenses, just not the little things." I asked if he could give an exact point at which he wanted to begin to split the cost. "Well, I don't know, maybe $400 or $500." I turned to Ellen, but she was shaking her head. "No way, not with that attitude." I explained that we needed to move on to a new issue as we had a lot to cover during this session. I did not express my feeling that this issue had become difficult to resolve now because of emotions. Sometimes mediating is knowing when it is best to move on. We would return to this at a later time.

The session continued with the division of the rest of their assets. I had barely introduced the subject of the pension when David said, "We've already decided that I'll get the pension. Ellen's already agreed to it." I explained that before any decision could be reached, each person needed the pertinent information. Regarding a marital asset, pertinent information definitely includes the value of the asset. David had been employed by the same company for sixteen years and his pension plan was almost certainly a substantial asset.

During the introductory meeting, both of them had been surprised to hear me describe the pension as a marital asset.

I offered this analogy: "Let's say that instead of a pension plan, your employer allowed you to contribute $50 per month to a special fund. You could take the money out of the fund whenever you wished. After eight years you take the money out and buy a new living room set. Ten years later you are getting a divorce. Who owns the living room set? The money used to buy the set is the same money that could have gone into a pension fund."

Indeed, for those long-term married couples with a company pension plan, the pension, rather than the house, is often their biggest asset. Only 11 percent of the U.S. work force, however, has a company pension, and in most states the inclusion of a pension as a marital asset has taken place only within the last few years.

David had brought in a description of his employee retirement benefit package. The projected monthly pension payments stated David would receive $2,288 per month at age sixty-five if he continued at his present rate of pay until that age.

We went over various pension options. I asked David what he wanted to do concerning the pension. "I don't want to be working in the future for a pension that Ellen will end up getting. I just don't think that's fair." I then asked him if he thought she should get any of the pension. "Well, she's only entitled to the pension I've earned during the years we were married."

I asked Ellen what she thought after reviewing the information concerning the pension. She said, "I had absolutely no idea that his pension was worth that amount of money. I didn't think that it was worth much and I just agreed with him that it was his. Now I think that I deserve something because the pension was for both of us. I don't see why his new wife should get it all. We used to joke about the day we'd go off in our Jeep across the country camping. David would say that our pension would give us enough money for gas and cigarettes." Ellen lowered her head and I could tell this was difficult for her. I waited a moment and said, "That must have been before the bad news from the Surgeon General about smoking." They both smiled at my little joke, but the laughter broke the tension and we were able to continue the pension discussion.

They decided that Ellen's share in the pension should be based on the years they were married, and used a formula that resulted in a 25 percent share of the pension for Ellen at David's retirement. Ellen would have her share of the pension changed to her name. They did not need to have the pension appraised now as they were dividing it in the future, rather than either one buying out the other's share now.

After resolving the pension, I moved on to their remaining assets. The first were the cars—assets that are usually easy to divide, especially if the cars are comparable in value. Ellen's was a 1987 Plymouth Reliant and David's was a 1986 Honda Accord.

The next asset was the stock that David had at his place of employment: they both wanted to divide the stock equally. We then moved on to discuss the bonds. The bonds were mature, and David suggested that they cash them in and divide the proceeds so they would each have more liquid funds.

We spent some time on life insurance, and David ended up keeping his whole life insurance policy, so he got the cash surrender value of approximately four hundred dollars. Since this is an asset (because there is a cash surrender value), we offset the insurance with the bonds. Ellen would therefore get four hundred dollars more from the bonds.

Ellen remains beneficiary of David's $104,000 group term life insurance policy as long as he is required to pay child support.

The division of assets was going along smoothly until we came to the area of bank accounts, which at the time had roughly five thousand dollars in them. David began, "I want a bigger share because I'm the one who has to go out and buy new furniture."

"So you think that I should give you more money so you can have new furniture while I get the old, broken-down furniture?" They argued for a short time before I asked David to tell us exactly how much was "a bigger share." He hesitated and then said he needed to think about it. I pointed out to them that it might actually be easier to argue over a specific amount of money rather than argue over the principle, as they were doing now. David cleared his throat and said, "I want to get $3,000 and have Ellen get $2,000." Ellen stared at him, "Well, what if we both get $2,500 and we split the furniture?" David turned his head in disgust. "Forget it. I thought you wanted all the furniture so the house wouldn't look empty."

The session time had run out, and the decision would have to be made next time. I suggested that they discuss the bank account division between themselves outside mediation and see how it went. Regarding the house contents, I asked if they each wanted to make a list of the items they wanted or if they preferred that one of them make a list, with the other person getting the remainder. They chose the latter, with David making a list of what he wanted to take. I suggested that he show Ellen the list during the week to see if she agreed to him taking the items listed, and they could bring in the list and discuss any disagreements next week.

Fifth Session

David arrived on time but was very quiet. Ellen arrived ten minutes late and was clearly angry. She glared at David, who looked past me as he had done in our early sessions. When I asked what had happened, David tersely replied, "She just won't stop insulting me."

Ellen yelled, "You just walk out the door and think you can continue telling me what to do. I'm sick and tired of you."

The fight was a familiar one. When David had come to the house for the children, he had knocked and waited to be invited in, as was his new pattern. Then apparently an old familiar pattern returned: he had walked around turning off lights and the TV set. We talked about letting go of old patterns of behavior and substituting new ones. I defused the anger and we began to work on the last of the settlement.

They had five areas left to settle: who would pay for house repairs, the division of their bank account, the division of their house contents, how they would handle college expenses for their children, and who would assume responsibility for charge card debt. I suggested we start with the educational expenses first. (I knew they were still angry over their argument, and education was a more productive subject for them to talk about at this time.)

Both Ellen and David hoped that their children would want to attend college, and both wanted to help pay the costs. Ellen said, "We both want the kids to go to college, so I thought we should each pay half of the college costs, but we want more information before we agree to it." (I was pleased to hear that their decision-making process now involved gathering information before making decisions.)

After some explanation and discussion, Ellen said, "I think that it would be fair if each of us paid according to how much money we are making."

David agreed, "I don't mind paying more if I'm making more. But what if one of the kids decides to go to Harvard? I mean, that might be great, but I don't want to have to spend every cent I have to pay for it." I asked Ellen if she agreed with his concerns, and since she did, they agreed to put limits on the amounts they'd each be responsible for. They wanted to put $600 in bonds toward educational costs, and each child had a bank account with roughly $500 that the parents would use toward college. Ellen would control the children's accounts.

We listed the exact college costs each would be responsible for. The agreement covered tuition, books, student fees, and travel expenses. They did not want to tie themselves down to room and board, though both felt they would certainly pay for it if they could afford it. David suggested the agreement state that they wanted their children to attempt to obtain scholarships and grants, and to contribute to their own college expenses.

Next, I had each of them list the debts that they would be responsible for. Credit card charges are usually an area of conflict. David and Ellen, as with many separated couples, still had joint credit cards, and they needed to make several decisions concerning the continued use of the cards and the responsibility for the payment of the outstanding balances. Ellen agreed to closing all the joint accounts but one. "I want to use the Master Charge until I can get my own card." David agreed that she'd have a hard time getting credit until she got a job. "I just want her to apply for her own card as soon as she can. And I know that she will, so it's fine with me." She agreed to be responsible for any charges she made, and David agreed not to use the card. David would close their other joint accounts.

I moved next to the issue of house repairs. Ellen said, "We reached a figure for repairs, though he made his usual nasty comments." She turned to David. "Is it still settled?" David nodded and turned to me. "We agreed that Ellen would pay for all repairs under $300 and that we would split the cost of any repairs over that amount." I looked at Ellen and she added, "Do you believe it—we actually came up with an agreement by ourselves!" I congratulated them heartily.

They had some difficulty resolving the division of the house contents, though they differed on only three items. We reviewed David's list; Ellen was not happy about him taking the VCR, the stereo, and the dining room set. Ellen turned to David. "You know that the kids use the VCR and the stereo. And the dining room would look empty without furniture. I just don't understand you." Though David seemed frustrated and tired, he did not lapse into his old silence. "Look, Ellen, I was the one who picked out our dining room set. You know how much I like it."

I could feel the tension in the room starting to rise. I told them we would discuss each item in dispute and that I wanted to know about the next item, the stereo. David explained, "I need it more than the kids do." Ellen rolled her eyes a bit, then said, "I know you used to play it more than the kids ever did. But now you're out all the time, so I don't see why you need it." I stopped the arguing and asked about the next item, the VCR.

After a very short discussion, David said, "Look, I'll leave the dining room set for a while, okay?" Ellen seemed intent. "I think it really belongs in the room, David."

We settled the stereo by spending some time talking

about what the children wanted or needed. Ellen said, "The kids can save and buy one if they really care." He would take the stereo with the rest of the items, which Ellen actually wanted out of the house as soon as possible. They agreed on a date by which David would have the dining room set.

The only item left was the VCR, and Ellen brought up the children's desire for the VCR. After minimal discussion, David said, "I know that Jeff uses it a lot. I'll leave it at the house for the kids. But it's mine after they leave."

Ellen looked at him as if he had gone mad. "What are you talking about? Do you expect it to last forever?"

"It will if you take care of it, Ellen."

"Well, I'm not going to be responsible for it. Just remember that. But I do think that Jeff wants to use it."

This division of the contents of the house is often a difficult one to negotiate outside of mediation. Sometimes it isn't all that easy in mediation.

This left only one more decision, the dividing of the funds in their joint bank account. After some discussion, Ellen said, "I just don't think it's fair if he ends up with brand-new furniture. And I'm sure as hell not going to pay for him to do it." David replied, "I don't intend to buy the best, Ellen, I just need a couch and a table and, well, you know, lamps and whatever."

I asked David how much money the furniture would cost. "I think around $1,000." Ellen felt that since she was getting most of their house furnishings, she would give David an extra $400 of their savings toward his furniture. Her suggestion meant a bank account division of $2,700 for David and $2,300 for Ellen. They both agreed to it.

This was the last of the agreements they had to reach as part of their settlement. They smiled and sighed with relief when I told them they wouldn't need a sixth working session. We set up their last appointment, at which time they would review their Memorandum of Understanding.

Final Session

We greeted one another with a certain familiarity. Ellen and David were formally polite to each other, but the icy overtones of their earlier sessions were gone. They took their accustomed seats with assurance and I gave each of them a copy of the Memorandum. They reviewed the document (see appendix II) and made two minor changes. Ellen gave an audible sigh of relief as we finished.

I signed the Memorandum and explained that they could sign the agreement at any time with or without a lawyer's review, or their lawyers could use the Memorandum as a basis for drafting a separation agreement. Once the document is signed, it is legally binding and may be then submitted to the court for the court's approval, whereupon it becomes part of the divorce decree.

I always end the mediation by asking my clients if they will give me their opinion of the mediation sessions, as well as any suggestions for change.

Ellen began, "It was the best way for us to do it. I think we would have had a terrible divorce if we had used lawyers and the courts. You might not know it"—Ellen laughed and continued—"well, maybe you do know that David and I can both be real fighters."

David jumped in quickly. "I told you we'd be better off this way."

Ellen didn't rise to the bait. "I really wasn't too sure about mediation. I thought I'd have to compromise a lot. Instead, I pretty much got what I wanted."

"So did I. And I knew mediation would be much less expensive. Why not keep the money for the kids and ourselves."

Ellen turned to look at him and sighed. "David, money is still all you care about."

I've heard of a mediator that serves champagne to his clients at their final session. Though I don't do this, I certainly share the feeling of having been part of a significant accomplishment. Two people have managed to work out a fair settlement while going their separate ways. We said our good-byes and I asked if I could call each of them in one year to find out how the agreements and the divorce had worked out. I told them to call me if there was any future concern with their settlement and wished them well.

5

Do You Still Have to Go to Court?

Divorce is a legal act that ends a marriage. Each state has its own unique set of separation and divorce laws that govern divorce within that state. Throughout most of the United States, however, both you and your spouse are required to appear in court to obtain your divorce.

Years ago, the road to divorce was fraught with difficulties. Even if both spouses agreed to end their marriage and reached a settlement of their assets, the law did not allow them to end their marriage without providing legal "grounds." Various types of marital misconduct were grounds for divorce, including physical cruelty, adultery, desertion, chronic drunkenness, institutionalization, and mental abuse. It wasn't enough to merely allege the grounds for divorce, a spouse also had to prove them to the satisfaction of the court. Couples often disagreed as to who would allege the grounds and how to prove them in court. If neither spouse had grounds for the divorce, they had only two choices, to lie in court or to remain in an unhappy marriage.

As recently as the 1960s, there were only a few states that had liberal divorce laws. These states were predominantly in the western part of the country; Nevada is the best known of these states. The majority of states had divorce laws that were so restrictive that even couples who had good reasons to divorce were prevented from legally ending their marriage. Janice Runsey, for example (not her real name), was thirty-one years old in 1959. She had been married to Bill Runsey for nine years but had lived with him for fewer than three years. During their short time together, Bill drank and beat her. Shortly after the birth of their second child, Bill beat their older child while in a drunken rage. Janice rushed her daughter to the hospital and never returned to Bill. She moved in with her parents and supported herself and her two children as best she could. Bill, never having had a steady job, started to drift around the country. Every once in a while he would call Janice to verbally abuse and threaten her; on two occasions he sent her small amounts of money.

Five years after leaving Bill, Janice began dating Scott. They wanted to marry; Janice was excited at the prospect of having a new home for herself and her children. Most people would agree that Janice had more than enough grounds to get divorced. On May 12, 1959, Janice went to see a divorce lawyer. She was told that as adultery was the only grounds for divorce in New York state, she would not be granted a divorce unless she could actually prove to a court that Bill was unfaithful. Scott eventually married another woman. Janice continued to hear from Bill less and less as the years went by.

On May 12, 1959, the same day that Janice was talking to a divorce lawyer, Eddie Fisher left a Las Vegas courtroom accompanied by his lawyer and a witness. He came out and told reporters that he had never been so nervous in his life as during the fifteen minutes he was in this courtroom. (It was actually twelve minutes.) Eddie had been granted a divorce from his wife, Debbie Reynolds. Judge Zenoff, who had granted the divorce, said that Eddie's charges against Mrs. Fisher were "more than adequate to qualify him for a divorce in the state of Nevada."

Proof that Eddie was a resident of Nevada was given by Nat Brandwine, an orchestra leader who testified to the court that he had seen Mr. Fisher every day for the past forty-four days, as they were both appearing at the Tropicana night club. Eddie only needed to be in Nevada for forty-two days to meet that state's six-week residency rule.

Like Eddie Fisher, there were couples who avoided their state divorce laws by going someplace else. Of course to do this people had to have time and money, since transportation and accommodations required both.

Even today, I am sometimes asked about the possibility of going out of state to expedite divorce. Though such a deal may sound appealing to you, wait a minute before you reach for the nearest phone to make your reservations. There are several obstacles in your path. First is the fact that your own state (the state you actually live in as a married couple) may not recognize the property division and support agreement of your out-of-state divorce. This may create a serious problem for you if you must appear in your state court in any legal action connected with your divorce. In addition, very often people need to go back to court. If you divorced in Nevada and needed to go back to court, you might have to go back to Nevada and establish residency all over again, going through another six weeks in order to return to the jurisdiction of a Nevada court.

Fortunately, changes in the divorce laws have made it easier to attain a divorce. All fifty states now have some form of no-fault divorce, so that divorcing men and women do not have to allege false grounds to end their marriages. Janice Runsey could have gotten a New York divorce after 1967, when that state finally changed the law that had limited the grounds for divorce to adultery.

Divorce laws continue to evolve. There is a new law on the horizon that may change the rule requiring husband and wife to appear in court for their divorce. As is often the case, California is setting the pace. The proposed legislation will enable Californians who have under ten thousand dollars in assets and who do not have children to get their divorce through the mail. Once this law passes on the West Coast, it will most likely make its way across the country. Eventually, we may see the time when people can file for a divorce by mail and not be required to appear in court. This legislation will probably take years before it becomes a reality in every state. Legislatures and courts do not rush into social reform; they tend to hang on to the old ways, however difficult they are for their citizens.

Court Procedure

Court procedure differs in every state and even within localities, but most divorce court systems follow this general process. The first step is called "filing." This is a fairly simple procedure once you determine the appropriate court in which to request your divorce. Two factors determine where you file: the appropriate court that hears divorce cases and the specific court that has jurisdiction over your residence. Courts that hear divorce cases may be called "family," "probate," or "domestic" court. Usually this court hears what are called family issues, such as divorces, juvenile offenses, and wills. The typical family court of the

1980s, however, deals predominantly with divorce. In some states, such as Florida, divorce cases are heard in the same courts and by the same judges who hear murders, rapes, and robberies.

The second factor in filing—determining which court has authority over you—depends on where you live. *Jurisdiction* is the legal word for your residence. It refers to the specific court that has the authority to hear and grant you a divorce; many states use county, town, or city as their jurisdictional criteria.

The next step in the divorce procedure is to schedule the day and time for your court hearing, which is referred to as the "appearance." Most states allow you to file yourself (this is called *pro se*) or to have a lawyer represent you. The actual time you stand before the judge's bench during your appearance may be as short as ten minutes for a no-fault, uncontested divorce. If, however, you are engaging in a contested divorce (where the parties cannot agree to a settlement), the length of time spent in court increases dramatically.

After your court appearance with a final settlement, you begin the official waiting period. Every state has a waiting period; it ranges from one month to two years. The intent of the waiting period seems to be to allow time for people to cool off and change their minds about getting divorced. If either party contacts the court during the waiting period, the divorce process comes to a halt. Within the last twenty years, the waiting period in most states has been shortened from one of years to one of months. It is doubtful that the waiting period has ever accounted for a substantial number of people staying married. Still, there's not much that you can do about the waiting period—except wait.

Many people assume that the day you go to court is your

divorce date. It isn't. Your divorce is final on the date you went to court including the waiting period (assuming that neither of you contacts the court to challenge the settlement). This final date is often referred to as the date of absolute divorce.

Mediation's Role in Divorce

Divorce itself has two parts: the difficult part is reaching the settlement; the routine part is the court procedure just described. Mediation helps in negotiating the settlement, whether it is the entire agreement or one or more issues within the settlement. The court procedure can either be done on your own (*pro se*) or through one or two lawyers. (There will be more on this issue in chapter 9.)

Mediation may be used at any point in the divorce procedure. Most individuals using private mediators do so before taking the first step in the court process, that is, the filing. This is not true of people using court-ordered mediation, as they are required to use mediation after they have started the court procedure. Mediation may also be used after the divorce, when ex-spouses are in a dispute over an issue arising from their divorce, such as who pays for the college expenses for their children or what happens to parenting schedules when one parent moves. Remember, the court does not step in when there is a change in your settlement unless one of you petitions the court.

Today, the legal act of divorce may be a civilized process if approached in a reasonable manner, with knowledge of available options, and without a desire for blood or revenge. After all is said and done, divorce court is still not a place where many of us will want to spend much time. It is possible to limit your court time to one short visit if you mediate your settlement before you get to court and file for a no-fault, uncontested divorce.

WHAT IS MANDATORY MEDIATION?

Mandatory mediation occurs when a state or local government passes a law that requires people to use mediation. It can also occur informally when a judge orders a divorcing couple to go to mediation.

Divorce courts have begun to require mediation because of four compelling reasons. The first concerns the backlog of cases waiting to be heard in the courts. As the number of divorces in the U.S. increase, courts are overwhelmed by the sheer number of cases waiting to be tried. Delays of months and even years are not uncommon. The courts have tried to solve this backlog problem in a variety of ways. One of the earliest attempts involved using "masters"—often retired judges who serve as decision makers. The masters' decisions are presented to the court and the judge in charge of the case usually accepts the decision of the master. A second method is a decision by an arbitrator or, as is more common, a panel of arbitrators. Their decision is usually binding, unless a court determines that the arbitration process was invalid. Unfortunately, these strategies did not work particularly well for divorce cases. Mediation, on the other hand, is the first alternative that has proven effective within the area of divorce.

A second reason for the passing of mandatory mediation laws is to ease the public burden of the cost of divorce. Building space, salaries for a host of court workers, and the reams of paperwork that runs the legal system continue to escalate. The Los Angeles mandatory custody mediation program was one of the first experimental court programs in the country. In its first year, 1978, it saved the Los Angeles courts $175,000. The legislature cited this public saving as one of the major reasons mandatory mediation was enacted into law.

A third reason has to do with the number of divorced people who return to court. Over one-half of all people standing before a divorce court judge are trying to change their settlement. This relitigation costs the courts more money and further burdens the system. Mediation reduces this problem by reducing the number of litigants who return to divorce court.

The fourth reason for mandating mediation is what I call the human concern, the concern for the psychological and emotional well-being of divorcing people and their children. Governments and courts are finally starting to address the emotional price of the court process and are considering whether there are less destructive ways to handle divorce. The practical side to this concern is the recognition that divorce creates stress, which increases illness and accidents, thereby increasing the need for medical, psychological, and other services. The amount of money necessary to fund these services is paid for by the public, either in money for these services or the cost of increased demands made upon our hospitals and agencies. The courts needed to stop the drain of spiraling divorce services. Mediation has been found to reduce the stress of divorce in a number of significant ways, thereby reducing the demand for related services.

Most judges favor mediation as a way to resolve disputes, though there are still some who have never heard of it. Experienced divorce court judges realize that an agreement lasts longer if the parties have had input into the final decisions. Mediation, however, is a new field, and it is possible that your judge will not understand the procedure of mediation. You can find out more about the attitude of the court personnel in your district by talking to divorce mediators in your area and by attending a divorce court session, which is usually open to the public.

Since mediation has only been on the scene for a decade, it is extraordinary that it has gained such widespread acceptance by the courts. Several states already have mandatory divorce mediation, mainly with regard to custody and visitation issues. These states are California, Connecticut, Delaware, Hawaii, Kansas, Kentucky, Maine, Massachusetts, New Mexico, North Carolina, Oregon, Utah, and Virginia. The following states do not recognize mediation, but they strongly encourage it: Alaska, Colorado, the District of Columbia, Florida, Indiana, Michigan, Ohio, Oklahoma, and Washington.

Mandatory mediation was originally used to resolve custody disputes over minor children, traditionally the most difficult type of conflict to resolve. Its high rate of success in this area has prompted the courts to order mediation to help settle custody and visitation disagreements. The legislatures and courts have been slower to recognize that the destructiveness of conflict in a divorce is not limited to child custody disputes. Yet disagreements surrounding who gets the house or how much child support is paid cause serious emotional trauma and could also be resolved in mediation. Only recently has mediation been employed by the courts in the financial areas of divorce.

Some individuals, including mediators, have mixed feelings about mandatory mediation. They object to forcing men and women to use mediation. However, as long as men and women are forced to use the courts to get a divorce, mediation may be the only way to make the courts respond in a more humane way to the problems facing divorcing men, women, and their children.

DO COURTS HAVE DIVORCE MEDIATORS?

When a state or locality requires mediation, the divorcing couple may be given a choice between a public mediator or a private mediator. The public mediator is usually a court employee; how much authority these mediators have over the agreements of the couples who come to them differs in each state. Some public mediators have the authority to make legally binding decisions, usually concerning custody and visitation. Others make formal recommendations to the court, which are enacted into a court order by the judge, unless there is some extraordinary reason not to. And a number of public mediators provide information about a case only if the judge requests it.

The title of a public mediator depends on state policy and custom. Their backgrounds vary even more than their titles. Some are civil service employees transferred from other court departments, while others are trained and experienced mental health professionals.

A serious concern in public mediation is in the area of confidentiality. A "privilege" is a legally private conversation that cannot be subpoenaed into court. If there is no confidentiality, what you say to the mediator or your spouse in mediation may be repeated in court. This is an important issue that has generated considerable controversy and concern. Some states provide public mediators total confidentiality with their clients, while other states do not. If you are concerned about the issues of confidentiality and decision making, you need to find out what the court laws are in your jurisdiction.

Another concern with mandatory mediation is the limited amount of time allotted. Public mediators average less than six hours in working out a divorce settlement, compared to ten hours averaged by private mediators. Because of limited court resources, this situation is difficult to improve. On the other hand, one virtue of public mediation is that the cost to a divorcing person may be free or based on a sliding fee scale. A sliding fee scale adjusts fees according to your income, so court programs may be more financially affordable for those with low incomes.

In many states that allow divorcing couples to choose between a public mediator and a private mediator, the court may even provide a referral list of private mediators. When a settlement has been reached through private mediation, the final Memorandum is simply given to a lawyer to file, or presented directly to the court.

Though each state with a mandatory mediation program is different, they have one common theme: they are not voluntary. Once you begin the court process, it is quite difficult to extricate yourself from the system. And once a judge makes a decision in your case, it is difficult to get the judgment changed. Still, public mediators are a new and important resource to help you achieve a settlement in your divorce.

WILL I GET A BETTER SETTLEMENT IF I GO TO TRIAL?

Occasionally someone asks me, "Won't I get the entire house if I go to court and tell the judge what my husband did?" or "Wouldn't a judge see that I couldn't pay that kind of child support and decrease it?" The men and women asking these questions have one characteristic in common— they have never appeared in a divorce court action. Men and women who have already been to court for a divorce know how unrealistic these questions are. They know that you rarely get a chance to tell your entire story in court and when you do get the opportunity to speak, the parts you think are essential often are not allowed into evidence. The court decision will most likely hinge on technical aspects that seem absurd to someone not versed in "the law."

Most people go to court for one reason—they believe the judge will decide in their favor. Rarely have I met anyone wanting to go to court who assumes they are destined to lose. In some ways, it is a tribute to each person's ability to convince themselves that "I will win once the judge hears what happened." Unfortunately, this naive view of the judge as a kind fatherly protector may not be what awaits you in court.

The actual goals of the judge, in fact, may differ radically from yours. Many divorce court judges share the sentiment of one judge who says, "If I see each of them walking out of court with their head down and looking sad, then I figure I made a pretty good decision." Since there is so much to lose, the court tries to see that neither side loses too badly.

The reality of a divorce court trial is that most litigants walk out of the courtroom feeling as if they have just been run over by a truck. Even the apparent winner rarely feels good. What looks like winning on the outside often doesn't feel good either because the spouse feels entitled to much more than what the court awarded or because he or she feels guilty. The winner may also find his or her enthusiasm dampened by the warning they hear from their lawyer to prepare for the next round, when their soon-to-be-ex-spouse may appeal the judge's decision. An appeal means another trial, more money, and, of course, the emotional trauma that seems to have no end.

There is another courtroom myth that dies hard, the myth that legal fees are paid for by the party who loses. In most U.S. courts, this is simply not true. Our system of common law rarely allows an award for legal fees. Whether you win or lose, you will most likely be picking up your lawyer's tab.

While I paint a discouraging picture of trials, I think that some people must go to court. Apart from those with unreasonable spouses, any divorce cases in which physical or sexual abuse plays a role should signal an immediate run to the court. Be prepared for court; find out the procedure, ask about your rights, and talk to others in the same situation concerning their experiences.

Fewer than 10 percent of divorced people go to trial. Choosing to go to trial in your divorce is not a decision to be made lightly. The typical dirty divorce story rarely gets you what you want in court. Courts have strict rules concerning what is allowed as evidence, and the sad truth is that the judge has usually heard it all before. Courtroom trials are not necessarily the great arbitrators of fairness that will make up for the unfairness of divorce—and life.

6

At What Stage of Divorce Should You Use Mediation?

Divorce is a transition with both physical and emotional stages. The physical stages are easier to describe, but even these are not as cut-and-dried as most people would surmise.

There are two physical stages to divorce: living together and living separately. I'll begin by describing the three ways in which divorcing couples live together. The first is one in which the couple functions in their roles as husband and wife—eating dinners together, watching TV, and engaging in sex with each other. Outside their apartment, they continue to socialize as a couple with their friends and acquaintances. One person may be talking separation or divorce, but the other does not believe the marriage will really end.

The second way of living together occurs when a couple coexists but does not function in the roles of husband and wife. One person considers himself or herself to be separated, while the other does not. Within the house, they may eat dinner separately and plan separate activities on weekends and evenings. If they have children, only one parent at a time engages in an activity with them. They have probably not yet told their children of their planned separation. Friends and relatives still see them as a couple—when they *do* see them, since socialization is usually kept to a bare minimum. But the couple still feels obligated to socialize, or at least one person does. Often in this sort of coexistence they are not having sexual relations, but this is not a rule, and there are certainly couples who continue having sexual relations with each other.

The final way of living together while separating is to have separate lives while in the same physical quarters. Both people consider themselves separated, but continue to stay together for a variety of reasons, the most common one their lack of agreement on who should move out. Financial reasons are another prime motive for continuing to reside together—neither can afford to move into another apartment or house. By now, each has confided their separation to their closest friends. It varies as to whether or not they have told their children. Typically, the couple is not having sex with each other; in fact, one or both individuals may be dating others.

After living together in one of these three ways, or in a succession of two or three of these, the couple physically separates. Many states require a period of time that spouses must live apart (which cannot be within the same house or apartment), in order to file for divorce.

Friends and family members are told of the separation, but coworkers and acquaintances may not be informed. If the couple has children they will have been informed of the separation, perhaps as one parent walked out the door.

There is another group of separating couples that live

apart on separate floors, functioning as two individual households within one house. Such an arrangement has become more visible within the last few years and does not fit neatly into the living together or living separately categories.

The importance of physical separation cannot be overstated. The physical act of separating is often the most dramatic message to the spouse that the relationship is over. This is significant, since usually one spouse does not want the divorce and is emotionally resisting the end of the relationship. It also serves as a statement to the outside world of the intention of at least one spouse to end the relationship. Not all separations end in divorce, but all divorced people separate.

Many people use mediation before their physical separation rather than waiting until after they separate. There are many reasons why this is preferable, including the following:

1. To help the couple sort out the preliminary issues for each of them: for example, who should move out and under what conditions.
2. To reduce emotional, as well as possible legal, consequences of abandonment.
3. To set reasonable support figures.
4. To avoid bad decisions, such as giving away the house or waiving pension rights.
5. To avoid illegal decisions, such as agreeing whom you will or will not spend time with.
6. To reduce stress, since there is a neutral third party intervening within the highly charged couple interactions.

7. To avoid illogical decisions, such as making inflexible parenting arrangements.

In the past, most divorcing couples began mediation after they separated, but more frequently now, husbands and wives are seeking divorce mediation to help them make sound decisions before they take the physical step of separation.

EMOTIONAL STAGES OF DIVORCE

Rarely is anyone prepared for the end of their marriage. This is as true for the person who asks for the divorce as it is for the spouse. It is not easy to end a relationship, and everyone goes through a period of emotional transition, which can be broken down into a series of stages.

Over the years, my work with separating and divorcing individuals has led me to observe five distinct emotional stages that comprise the divorce transition. These combined stages last an average of three years; for some people the period is shorter, while for others it is longer. The stages usually occur in a specific order, though at times they may blend and overlap. Occasionally someone skips a stage, but this is rare.

The person who wants the divorce begins the first stage while still living with the spouse. This is usually not true for their spouse, who generally begins the first stage after the couple have physically separated. This difference in the beginning of the divorce transition, along with a natural difference in the length of time it takes each person to complete a stage, explains why spouses are invariably at different stages as they progress through the divorce. This difference adds to the communication gap between them.

Stage 1. Blaming the Spouse

The focus during this stage is on the spouse. You blame him or her for all the problems that are going on and have gone on in your life. Other personal concerns, such as growing old, career advancement, money, parenting, older parents, and health, don't get addressed as separate concerns, but rather as outgrowths of the problems believed to be caused by your spouse.

During this stage, both men and women are obsessively preoccupied with their past marital relationship. You may find yourself reliving scenes from the early years of your marriage and may answer questions about the present with a reference to your relationship in earlier times. For example, during a session with Bob and Janet, we were discussing how they wanted to divide their furniture, and I asked Bob about their leather couch, an item they were in disagreement over. He responded sadly, "All I can think of is the day we went to buy it. She took my hand and told me how much she loved me. Of course, it doesn't matter now."

During Stage 1, you may develop a negative self-image and be easily hurt. You may be depressed much of the time and experience a low energy level. To friends and relatives, you may seem to be too emotional or to be emotionally drained or blunted. You may have a constant swing of moods, with changing emotional tones. You express these feelings most strongly in your interactions with your spouse.

The characteristics of a person in Stage 1 differ depending on whether you are the initiator, that is, the spouse who asks for the divorce, or the noninitiator. If you are the initiator, you are seeking relief from a stressful situation. You have made your decision, and this act gives you momentary relief. Typically you experience guilt over your decision to divorce but you try to hide these feelings from your spouse. Your spouse sees you as being stubborn or going through a temporary aberration. As the initiator, you may be unwilling to continue working on the marriage. "There just isn't anything he can do that will make me stay married," is something I hear frequently from initiators during the early sessions of mediation. Your feelings of blame, fear, anger, and depression are often masked as you try to act naturally.

Sometimes the initiator is not the one who really wants the divorce. For example, Tom knew that if he continued his affair with Susan, his wife Barbara would end their marriage. He continued to see Susan and left evidence of his affair—motel room bills and restaurant receipts—where his wife would come upon them. Barbara finally told him that she couldn't stand it anymore and wanted a divorce. She may appear to be the initiator to the outside world, but it is Tom who wants out of the marriage.

The spouse who is not asking for the divorce is called the noninitiator. As the noninitiator, you feel out of control over the decision to divorce, and as a result you feel extremely helpless. You may react in one of two extreme ways: by letting your spouse make all the decisions or by taking control and making every decision.

Stage 1 marks the first time the noninitiator hears that the relationship is over. A period of disbelief, with a denial of the reality of the separation, begins. You may become a divorce opposer, spending all your energy fighting the divorce. You feel angry because you assume that your spouse is not in pain; you do not realize that the initiator was feeling pain earlier when he or she was in Stage 1. The predominant feeling suffered by the noninitiator is rejection, which leads to low self-esteem.

This stage is the most difficult of the stages because of the profound changes, loss, and fear of the unknown. It is as though the very foundation of life has shifted. A former client described this as "my shell shock months."

This is also a time of diminished parenting. Men and women are too deeply immersed in their own feelings to attend well to the needs of their children.

Stage 2. Mourning the Loss

This stage can be compared to the stages of death and dying elucidated by Elisabeth Kübler-Ross. The primary focus is acknowledging the end of the relationship. Anyone who has witnessed someone in this stage is struck by the profound grieving. "I just sat and cried for weeks" is not an exaggeration. The grief feels overwhelming.

Women are often depressed during this period. The depression, unlike sadness, encompasses a personal sense of failure, as if some part of it is one's fault. The sad feelings during this stage are different from those experienced during the earlier stage. The feelings of Stage 1 revolved around the spouse's opinion of you, but now the focus is on yourself. There is an exaggerated "poor me" attitude.

You may feel an overwhelming sense of melancholy as you relive scenes from earlier days—but as shaded by a different outcome. The future looms ahead, hopeless and meaningless. You may act out your depression by working harder or by drinking.

The newly separated have lost the anchor of people and homes around which they built their lives. The sense of loss extends to things as well as to people. Since it is men who often move out of the house (though this is less frequently the rule), they often experience a longing for furnishings as well as people, and yearn to sit once again in their favorite blue corduroy armchair.

Each of us builds our identity through the roles in our life. We each have several roles, which bear varying degrees of importance to us. The various roles of a divorcing woman, for example, may be those of mother, wife, daughter, veterinarian, friend, and bridge-player. Of a man, the roles may be father, husband, bank manager, neighbor, golfing buddy, and son. The impact of the loss of a role depends on how much the role means to you. A woman who derives her identity primarily from her role as a homemaker and who loses this role through separation will experience a diminished sense of herself. A client of mine described how she felt as she looked at her mail, addressed to Mrs. Frank Rossi, "That's not me anymore. I don't know who I am now." Employed men and women often have an advantage in that their identity as a worker remains consistent throughout their separation.

While in Stage 2, you may become overly sensitive or preoccupied with yourself. You need emotional support, yet are ambivalent about what you want. Often you demand conflicting responses from others, wanting both encouragement to save the marriage as well as support to end it.

A common problem for the separating man or woman is the actions of friends who mean well but who are insensitive to what the divorcing person is feeling, commenting, for example, "It isn't the end of the world." To you it *is* the end of the world. Such responses make you feel more misunderstood and isolated.

While in Stage 2, you may have difficulty concentrating on tasks as you are lost in a world of feelings, which may include crying spells and long silences. This preoccupation with your feelings does not translate well into parenting. You may hold onto a child in an attempt to recapture the spouse or behave in a rejecting manner to the child because of perceived similarities to the spouse. It is important to keep in mind that this period will pass. The children will survive, and you will move on to another stage.

For the first time since the transition from marriage, men and women are starting to realize that they may not be able to get what they want or need from their spouse. Most people would gladly skip this stage if they could, yet you must experience these feelings if you are to get on with your life in an emotionally healthy way.

Stage 3. Anger

Rage comes from a feeling of being betrayed—by your spouse, by life itself. It is a deep, dark, intense anger that colors every part of your being. Though anger is seen at just about every stage of the divorce transition, it is now the dominant trait. There is a sense of righteousness to the anger, that the spouse is wrong and deserves to suffer. A fantasy during this stage is that the judge will proclaim your spouse the bad guy—and you the wronged spouse.

This rage is often upsetting to family and friends, for they feel forced to take sides. They may actually feed your feelings of revenge and distrust with comments such as "I knew he was a bastard all along," or "I told you never to marry her." Though friends may even encourage the anger, they are wary of it and tend to shy away from the strong rage that is part and parcel of this stage.

People experience varying levels of anger and express it in a wide variety of ways. The anger is most often directed toward the spouse, but it may also be aimed at "all women" or "all men." Behind the feelings are many fears, among them, "How will I live alone? Will I have enough money to support myself?" These two most common fears—the fear of being alone and fear of lack of money—pervade all life-styles. Men may fear ending up in a windowless room at the YMCA. Women often say, "I'm so afraid I won't have enough money to pay my bills." Other fears soon begin to surface, such as, "How will I ever face people again?"

If you have never handled money, you may experience the fear of not having enough money most intensely. Overall, however, the feeling of helplessness is not as pervasive as during the earlier stages. Your fears are more specific and do not encompass your entire world.

Your anger at your spouse is usually of the "he or she never really understood me" nature. You're probably left feeling utterly alone. If you have primary physical custody of your children, you may have some protection from these feelings. Parents without physical custody of their children oftentimes fill the void with other relationships.

Parenting skills are returning, and you are better able to attend to the needs of your children. However, you may upset your children by reacting with a sudden, unexpected rage at the mention of your spouse. In general, your anger may confuse your children.

Your energy level is mixed, but for the first time during

the transition of divorce, there are more high periods than low ones.

Do not regard your anger as merely a negative characteristic; on the contrary, it serves an important function by helping you let go of the marriage.

Stage 4. Being Single

This is the stage that the media label as "second adolescence," since individuals are frequently trying out new experiences. Contrary to popular belief, these activities are not predominantly sexual. Though they may include such exciting adventures as white water rafting and hang gliding, for most people the changes will be much less dramatic. They may involve such "new" activities as watching Tom Brokaw deliver the evening news instead of Dan Rather. A woman may change the brand of coffee she's sworn by for the past fifteen years, or she may become the jogging novice of her neighborhood. A man may suddenly stop shaving and grow a beard, or he may become a gourmet cook, when once he thought boiling an egg was a culinary feat.

For many people, this is the first time in their lives that they have been single. Many went from mom and dad to marriage without ever living on their own. Single parents— and over 90 percent of these are women—do not experience this single state in the same way as persons without children, but they still have the new experience of making decisions without input from another adult.

For most men and women, the pressure to be a successful single is just that—pressure. Many will be having their first "date" in ten to twenty years, and it is an anxiety-provoking event. It is threatening to prove yourself in a world that not only has new rules, but also feels like an entirely new game. The solutions that worked years ago are often not suited to today's problems. The arena of sexual relationships is often more threatening than exciting, and even talking about sex is fraught with anxiety. Suddenly you are thrust into a world where you are even expected to discuss sexual details with strangers, if only to weed out the probability of sexually transmitted disease. Not easy conversation for someone who hasn't been on a date in fifteen years!

Being single, however, probably has more to do with making your own decisions and living on your own than it does with dating. You will feel an openness to meeting new people and discovering new activities. Often your spouse will be upset to learn that the new activity is something he or she has wanted you to share with them. Over the years, a woman desperately wanted her husband to dance with her during their married years, but he always refused. Some months after their separation, she heard from friends that he was out dancing every Saturday night. Another man wanted his wife to go camping. She insisted that she simply could not survive such an experience, yet shortly after their separation he heard that she had spent her vacation in a tent in the Smoky Mountains. Divorced people will tell you many similar stories.

The active change in behavior during this stage confuses friends and relatives. Though they feel glad that you are out of your slump, they fear what they view as extreme behavior. Friends yearn for the return of their old friend as they once knew you. This is a difficult time for relationships, for neither person has a sense of when the divorced person will settle down, or what he or she will be like.

Another problem with maintaining friendships during this time is that friends may be forced to deal with the state of their own marriage. Your separation may bring up issues of their own marriage that they may not want to deal with.

There are a multitude of positive changes taking place in you during this stage. One of the most significant is your growing sense of being a whole person, of not needing your spouse to make you complete. You are starting to feel good about your decision to end the marriage, and are starting to trust in yourself to make other decisions.

Parenting tends to reestablish itself at this stage, as you begin to feel that you can now provide nurturing to your children after the confusion of the past. However, there is one troublesome aspect. If you are the parent of adolescents, you may have a very difficult time, as these children tend to be harshly judgmental of any behavior they see as immoral in their parents. The adolescent will strongly condemn his parents for not living according to his conception of how a parent should act. It is a rare adult who is prepared for the moral wrath of the adolescent daughter or son!

Your focus at this stage is on yourself and on your relationships with people in your life. You will feel able to make decisions concerning the present and the near future. You won't feel comfortable making a commitment to coach soccer for three years, but you will feel fine making a decision to play for one season.

You'll find that your self-image is much improved and is actually positive. You basically look to yourself to fulfill your own needs and wants. Whether you are a man or a woman, you are building new support systems as well as starting new activities.

You will probably find yourself ready to begin facing your personal issues—sexuality, aging, parents, and work. You have energy for a variety of life's tasks and are no longer stuck hashing over the past relationship with your spouse.

If you are in another significant relationship before completing the stages of divorce, you may miss much of the positive aspects of this stage, which is the sense of confidence in yourself. Though it may feel good to have a lover feel good about you, in the long run it is more valuable for *you* to be the one who feels good about you!

Your energy level will usually be fairly high, especially coming as it does after stages of low energy. You will still feel ambivalence during this stage, but there are more ups than downs.

Stage 5. Reentry

The fifth and last stage of the divorce process is a time of settling down. Men and women alike believe that they have some degree of control over their future. You feel better about yourself: you are able to make decisions easily and to commit to long-term as well as short-term plans. You have confidence in your ability to make rational decisions. If there is a predominant theme during Stage 5, it is this feeling of being in control of your life again.

You will find that your interactions with people are no longer restricted to new acquaintances. Activities reflect this change: new routines have developed, and you may have gone back to some old ways. Life has settled down by now.

You will still have strong feelings toward your ex-spouse,

but they do not dominate your life. You are accepting the end of your marriage and are capable of going on with your changed life.

Virtually every divorcing man and woman goes through these five stages to be able to put divorce behind them and get on with life. The sad individuals are those who do not seem to reach the latter stages. Unable to let go of their old lives, they remain rooted in bitterness and wounded pride. How many of you recognize the woman eternally recounting the story of the day her husband ran off and left her? Doesn't it make you want to shout, "Enough is enough. Get on with your life." Most individuals will successfully pass through the stages of divorce and proceed from there. Many are apt to be a little wiser and more thoughtful from the experience and are better able to take control of their changed lives.

During which emotional stage of divorce should you mediate? The emotional stages you and your spouse are in will greatly influence your mediation.

Stage 1, Blaming the Spouse, is noted for its negative focus on the other person. You feel that you have very little control over your life, especially if you are the spouse who doesn't want the divorce. The adversarial arena is painfully difficult during this time, as it feels as though other people are making all of your decisions. In contrast, mediation allows you and your spouse to take some degree of control over your lives and to start making short-term decisions concerning your physical separation.

Divorcing men and women need information to make decisions about the present, but should not, at this stage, be pressed to make decisions concerning their future. Mediation encourages tasks that are geared for this period and helps to stabilize and make sense of the ambivalent feelings that are prevalent.

Stage 2, Mourning the Loss, is the time during the divorce transition in which individuals feel most acutely the pain of their separation. If you are in an adversarial setting during this time, you often feel torn in two conflicting directions. The grief doesn't fit in with the pressure to defeat your spouse. The adversarial environment does not allow for grief, rather it fans the fires of anger. Therapists say that grief is anger turned inward; the adversarial forum propels people to the next stage of anger before they have mourned the end of their marriage.

In spite of their sadness, people at this stage are able to reach agreements in mediation more easily than during the first stage. Positive feelings toward the spouse surface and serve to establish a necessary foundation for people to work out what's best for each of them. Practically, mediation helps the feelings to be constructively channeled into a framework that allows for a fair settlement.

Stage 3, Anger, is the most dangerous time to be using the adversarial court system. Divorcing men and women are easy prey for the winner-take-all attitude that typifies divorce litigation. Years of Perry Mason come flooding back, and someone's anger can easily transform him into an angry divorce litigant. If you hear of a bitter, hotly contested divorce trial, you can be certain that at least one of the spouses is in the anger stage.

Mediation plays the most significant role during this stage by defusing the anger. Rather than fuel the fire, it redirects energy by focusing on concrete and specific aspects of the short- and long-range details of the agreements. When you are in this stage you have a fairly high energy level and can actively take part in the divorce discussions. You are able to be quite productive.

Stage 4, Being Single, is a safer stage for divorcing people to be caught in the adversarial arena than any of the preceding stages. You are more in control of your emotions and not so easily led by your feelings. Just the same, you will feel enormously frustrated by the legal maneuvering as you seek to resume taking charge of your life. Your attempt to be single in the area of relationships with others may actually be met with punishment by the courts.

This stage is an ideal time for mediation, primarily due to the newly emerging positive attitude one has toward change. You are open to the various problem-solving solutions that are discussed in mediation. Because you are starting to feel good about yourself, you can be sensitive to someone else's point of view—even your spouse's. Mediation is easier and quicker if at least one person is in the stage of Being Single.

Stage 5, Reentry, is the last stage of the divorce process. If both spouses are in this stage, they will rarely be engaged in a courtroom trial. However, since it takes two people to fight or to agree, if one person is at an earlier stage, it may be difficult for the spouse who is in the reentry stage to avoid a battle.

Individuals in Stage 5 feel fairly good about themselves and are able to make long-term plans and commitments. By this point, people have generally completed their divorce settlement and the agreements have been finalized.

As you see, mediation can be used during any of the physical and emotional stages of divorce. It is especially helpful during the earlier stages of separation in order to avoid future problems and the dangers of the adversarial system.

WHY WOULD YOU USE MEDIATION *AFTER* YOUR DIVORCE?

On November 13, 1789, Benjamin Franklin penned these immortal words: "In this world nothing is certain but death and taxes." Obviously Mr. Franklin was not a divorced person who had children, owned property jointly, or was sending or receiving support. If he had been, a certainty he would have added was continuing problems with an ex-spouse.

In my experience, men and women who request mediation after divorce come to resolve three primary problems: conflict around their minor children, joint ownership of their marital residence, and a request for a change in alimony payments.

A frequent dispute around children concerns who will pay college expenses. Years ago, it was not common practice to include such a provision in a divorce agreement, and years later, divorced parents would struggle over how to pay for college. Nowadays, more divorce agreements address college expenses, yet it is often difficult to make these financial decisions when your children are still toddlers.

Another conflict around children frequently arises if one parent plans to move out of state. No amount of preliminary planning can obviate the need to discuss new parenting arrangements at the time of the move.

Other conflicts surrounding children peak immediately after the divorce and tend to diminish with time. Disputes about children concern changes in the visitation schedules, child-rearing practices (especially when the children begin driving and dating), and stepparenting influences. Probably the best-known conflict focuses around child support payments, though these disagreements are more likely to end up in court than in a mediator's office. Other disagreements surrounding children are in the areas of medical and dental expenses, especially the cost of orthodontics.

Continuing joint real estate ownership—usually the marital house—is another major reason why divorced people use mediation after their divorce. A typical case involved Linda, who wanted to add a larger deck to the house she still jointly owned with her ex-husband Steve. He was adamant in not wanting to add the deck, as their divorce decree called for them to split equally the cost of improvements. If you change names and details, the scenario is familiar to every divorced couple who has continued joint ownership of their house. And this is one issue that is often aggravated by time. The individual living in the house typically wants to make more changes to the house, while the person not residing in the house becomes more reluctant to pay for improvements.

Another real estate conflict that may be resolved through mediation occurs when an ex-spouse wants to buy the other out of their equity in the house. One couple had owned their house together for three years after their divorce, and their divorce agreement gave her seven more years to live in the house before she had to sell it and split the proceeds with her ex-husband. She decided to buy him out now, and he wanted her to, but they couldn't agree on the financial specifics.

A property conflict that I see fairly often involves family-owned businesses. The marriage may end, but the business relationship continues. This sort of postdivorce mediation generally calls for a mediator with a high degree of business expertise.

The last type of dispute that often necessitates a mediator after the divorce is alimony payments. Typically a disagreement occurs because of the changed financial circumstances of either party: either the individual making the payments wants a reduction or the recipient wants more money.

Postdivorce mediation is an opportunity to resolve new and unanticipated conflicts without court intervention.

7

How Much
Does Mediation Cost?

It is still too early in the history of divorce mediation for national statistics on the cost of mediated settlements to have been gathered. Estimates do exist, however, based on research and practice. There are three significant factors that must be taken into account in determining the cost of a mediated settlement: the cost of living for the area, the mediator's professional background, and a profile of the divorcing husband and wife.

This chapter will focus on the cost of using a private mediator, rather than a court employee who is a public mediator. A rule of thumb is that mediation will cost you one-tenth the price of an adversarial divorce, but let's look at the specifics.

Most mediators have their practices in urban areas and charge fees that range from $60 to $200 an hour. What is probably surprising about this figure is that the lower end of the range is more common than the higher end. I'll explain why later in this chapter.

The mediation rate outside the cities and their suburbs is more difficult to measure because there are relatively few mediators in rural areas. Fees are lower, ranging from $35 to $60 an hour.

What you pay can also depend on whether the mediator, or the agency that employs the mediator, has a sliding fee scale. Some agencies may even provide free services to those who cannot afford them.

A majority of all mediators come from the field of mental health, and their rates often reflect their professional background. As a result, most urban mediators charge between $70 and $100 per hour, reflecting the going rate for therapists and psychologists in urban locations.

The higher end of the rate scale—from $150 to $200 per hour—is more often the fee charged by mediators who are lawyers. These practitioners tend to bill at their hourly legal rate, which in most areas is higher than therapist rates.

A fee arrangement that is not appropriate for mediators is a contingency fee. This type of arrangement, commonly used by lawyers in automobile liability claims, has the professional take a percentage of the settlement. Contingency fees are common in personal injury cases. (For example, assume that a woman is injured in a car accident and receives a settlement of $20,000; under a 40-percent contingency fee arrangement, the lawyer would take 40 percent of the settlement, or $8,000.) I can't stress enough that a contingency fee arrangement is not appropriate for mediation.

Another important feature you may run into during a description of fees is the use of a "retainer." This is up-front money and is a quite common fee arrangement for lawyers. It works this way: the professional may request a $1,000 retainer; and if the rate is $100 per hour, this means that you are paying in advance for ten hours of work. Most mediators do not ask for retainers, but again the exception to this are mediators who are lawyers. Retainers are not, in and of themselves, a bad idea, but they do tend to limit your freedom to leave the mediation since you have already paid for services.

Virtually all mediators charge by the hour. Indeed, most local and national professional mediation organizations have a rule stating that the mediator must charge by the hour.

The average number of hours in a mediated settlement is ten. The average mediation fee of $85 an hour brings the total cost to $850. This price is not a per-person amount, as it would be with a lawyer. This $850 is the mediation cost for sessions for both people.

There may be other costs in your mediation, such as the final cost of the Memorandum of Understanding. Some mediators incorporate this cost into their hourly rate, while others charge a separate fee for the written Memorandum. Other charges may be phone calls, documentation review, and consultations with other professionals. The average mediated divorce settlement costs a little under $1,000.

The cost of a traditional adversarial divorce in cities and other fairly expensive locations is roughly $6,000 per person. If you are in a rural area, with few assets, and using local attorneys, your costs will most likely be less—roughly $3,000 to $4,000. Compare these figures with mediation costs of under $1,000!

We have looked at two of the three factors that determine the costs of mediation: the cost of living in your area and the background of the mediator. But the remaining factor—the profile of the divorcing couple—is by far the most important determinant of the savings involved in using mediation as opposed to an adversarial procedure.

HOW MUCH WILL YOU SAVE USING MEDIATION?

In 1981, the average price of a typical middle-income divorce was slightly under $2,000 per person, for a total of $4,000. The average price is now approximately $6,000 per person, for a total of $12,000. Divorce costs are skyrocketing, and there are no signs of their leveling off.

A mediated divorce can save you money in three significant ways. The first is the savings of the cost of mediation compared to the cost of using the adversarial process, the second is the money saved by not returning to court, and the third is the money saved by not having to pay for services incurred as a result of the high stress of divorce.

There are other factors that affect your savings in a mediated divorce. The two most significant ones are the divorcing couple's behavior and the amount of money they have.

In order to determine exactly how much you can save, you need to determine first which Money group and which Behavior group you belong to. There are three categories in the Money group, which correspond to a couple's total income and assets. They are:

Wealthy: Combined annual income of over $150,000 or assets of $500,000 or more.

Middle-income: Combined annual income between $20,000 and $149,000 and assets from $10,000 to $500,000.

Low-income: Combined annual income under $20,000 and assets under $10,000.

Next, determine which Behavior group each of you belongs to. (These groups do not describe whether you want or do not want a divorce.) There are two categories of Behavior: Fair and Vengeful.

Behavior plays a crucial role in divorce settlements because of self-fulfilling prophecy. This concept means that your expectations of the future influence results. Thus, individuals who expect to reach a settlement have a high probability of doing so, and people who expect to wage a divorce war are likely to find themselves in the midst of a battle on every issue in their settlement.

When you are considering which category you are in, keep in mind that having differences over what you each want still allows you to remain in the Fair category. Differences do not mean that you belong in the Vengeful group.

The Fair settlement category includes both those couples who agree with each other and those who do not. But, whereas the men and women in the Fair category may feel hurt and angry, they do not play out their emotions within the divorce settlement.

The Vengeful category is composed of those who use revenge as a main focus of their settlement. It is exhibited by these types of divorcing behavior: emptying the joint savings account, making outrageous charges on charge cards, stopping support checks, and leaving the state with no forwarding address. Stories such as these terrify separating people, who fear that their spouse will suddenly turn to revenge. Probably the most disturbing aspect of this group is that even if only one of the spouses is set on Vengeful behavior, the couple falls into the Vengeful group. Also, if you don't embark on such behavior but your lawyer does, you will have pushed your divorce into the Vengeful category.

Let's take a look at the groups of divorcing people based on our two factors, Money and Behavior.

- Fair and Wealthy
- Fair and Middle-income
- Fair and Low-income
- Vengeful and Wealthy
- Vengeful and Middle-income
- Vengeful and Low-income

Fair and Wealthy

The average adversarial divorce for a wealthy couple costs more than it does for couples with a more limited income. The individuals in this category would spend approximately $15,000 per person in legal fees. This is not true for a mediated divorce. Mediators charge by the hour, not by the income and assets of the divorcing couple. Their mediation costs will average the usual $1,000 per couple. They will most likely have expenses for other professionals, such as tax and financial consultants. The adversarial cost of $30,000 is thirty times the mediated cost of $1,000.

Fair and Middle-income

This is the typical middle-class divorcing couple in America today. They will agree on some divorce issues and disagree over others. Their adversarial divorce will cost approximately $6,000 each, for a total of $12,000. Their mediation cost is $1,000, which provides a savings of $11,000 for a mediated divorce.

Fair and Low-income

Divorcing couples in the third group exhibit the same behavior but have much less income and fewer assets. The cost of a divorce falls hardest on these men and women. If neither party can borrow extra money to pay for divorce costs, they may simply live apart until their financial picture changes and they become able to afford a divorce. Federal and state domestic legal aid services for low-income people have been all but abolished. Because of their reduced financial circumstances, their financial negotiations should be less complicated, and their mediation costs well under $1,000.

Those couples in the Vengeful behavior group will most likely have mediations that cost more than that of Fair couples. Many of these couples have been to court and are still arguing; others have already exhibited behavior where one spouse has antagonized the other, such as hiring a sheriff to serve a summons, changing locks on doors, or emptying bank accounts. These divorcing husbands and wives will need one-and-one-half to two times the number of mediation sessions, so their cost may be $1,500 to $2,000. It probably won't go that high, but let's look at the savings involved using the higher figure.

Vengeful and Wealthy

The wealthy couple has an annual income of at least $150,000. They will continue their fighting to the courtroom steps if they do not use mediation. They have the money to wage all-out divorce battles, and there are scores of lawyers waiting to be hired as their gladiators. Included in this group are wealthy celebrities whose messy divorce battles make front-page news.

Each person in this group will average $35,000 in legal fees, for a total of $70,000. The cost of mediation for a

Vengeful couple (and remember, one vengeful individual makes such a couple) is $2,000. They have the potential of saving the extraordinary amount of $68,000 by using mediation instead of the adversarial system.

Vengeful and Middle-income

There is a wide range of income and assets for this group, and the average cost of a divorce depends on income and assets as well as behavior. In couples with annual incomes of $20,000 to $149,000 and assets of $10,000 to $500,000, where one or both spouses is out for blood, the price of divorce varies the most. The average cost is $15,000 for each person, for a total of $30,000 for the couple. Their revenge motivation may double the usual mediation cost to $2,000. The difference between $30,000 and $2,000 gives them a savings of $28,000.

Vengeful and Low-income

This last group includes couples in which one or both spouses want to fight over their divorce settlement but don't have the money to do so. This group must first find the money to wage a courtroom battle. It is unlikely they will have any savings for legal fees; what savings they may have will soon be eaten up, as they need at least $2,000 each to contest the divorce. Their savings will be whatever amount of money they might spend over $2,000.

In addition to the initial savings just described, the savings involved by not returning to court are significant. Half of all divorcing people who do not use mediation return to court. Mediated agreements do not have such dismal failure rates. In fact, studies have shown 90-percent-plus compliance rates.

Many couples who will choose mediation will also save on the other costs that accompany the emotional trauma accented in an adversarial divorce. Stress and trauma increase the probability of requiring medical attention, seeking therapy, using medication, losing time from work, and reducing work capacity. This can translate into financial savings—reduced stress and trauma means a reduction in these costs.

WHAT IF YOU DON'T HAVE ANY MONEY?

While speaking at a forum on negotiating divorce agreements, a man came up to me and asked, "How can I use mediation if I don't have any money?" I think it's an important question and would like to offer some suggestions for mediation when lack of money is the primary obstacle.

There are several options available with private mediators. Since many are mental health professionals, they are often accustomed to charging fees based on a sliding scale. This sliding scale takes your income into account, so the fees charged correspond to what you can afford. A mental health or community agency may offer sliding fee scales or reduced fees, as these agencies may receive state or local funding and may be able to pass on lower rates to you. It is always a good idea to ask about fees before you meet with a professional you may hire.

A second option is to ask the mediator to set up a payment plan. Many professionals require payment at the time of service, but many mediators working with divorcing clients realize that their situation may not allow them to make immediate full payment. If you can make such arrangements, it will allow you to budget your mediation costs in the same way that you pay many of your other bills.

Another alternative is to ask the mediator if he or she is willing to negotiate the fees. Many mediators, though they may not have formal sliding fee adjustments, nevertheless will adjust payments according to your available income and assets. You never know until you ask.

Still another possibility, though much less common than the preceding options, is that a mediator may take a case *pro bono*, in other words, for free. Pro bono mediation services are, unfortunately, not abundantly available.

There are other mediation resources that are not private. One such possibility is a community mediation center, which may be available in urban areas.

Another option for couples with limited financial resources is court public mediators. Though most people prefer to avoid the court system if at all possible, court mediators should not be overlooked. If you do decide to use court mediators, take a good look at what the court calls mediation. Does the mediator make the decisions for you? Is this decision binding? Is there confidentiality? Can you end the mediation at any time? Does the mediator make a recommendation to the court? These are some of the questions that you will want answered before using a court mediator.

Make no mistake about it, it costs money to get divorced. Years ago a common way to end a marriage was referred to as "the poor man's divorce"—a spouse simply walked away from the family. Formal, legal divorce was once the province of the rich. Divorce is now within the means of middle-income Americans, though a cartoon I saw recently may summarize the American attitude toward the cost of divorce today. It pictures the typical family after divorce. The "Woman after divorce" drawing shows a disheveled woman next to a small VW, an old, decrepit house looming in the background, and two kids hanging onto the hem of her dress. The "Man after divorce" drawing pictures a beaten-looking man standing in front of an old, rusted car, with a small, ripped suitcase in front of him, holding his empty pockets inside out. The last drawing is captioned "Lawyer after divorce" and shows a well-dressed man standing next to a shiny new Mercedes in front of a white-pillared mansion.

Whether you have no money, a limited amount, or considerable assets, you most likely do not want to spend it on the legal drama called "Divorce Court." Mediation can help you avoid the adversarial drama and expense.

8

How Do You Choose a Mediator?

The success of your divorce mediation will be greatly affected by your choice of a mediator. This chapter explores the qualifications you'll want to look for when choosing a mediator.

A mediator is a professional who intervenes between two or more parties to assist them in reaching an agreement. Mediators work in a variety of settings; you may be familiar with the work of labor mediators, for example, since labor disputes are widely reported in newspapers. The practice of mediation is unique in its multidisciplinary approach. Mediators borrow the best from the fields of psychology, law, financial planning, and negotiation. As a professional group, they have a high level of education, with the vast majority holding graduate degrees in the fields of social work, psychology, or law.

Two-thirds of divorce mediators come from the mental health fields of psychology, counseling, social work, and therapy; 19 percent come from a variety of other professions or from a different area of mediation; and 15 percent are lawyers. The appropriateness of lawyers acting as mediators is a controversial issue within the legal field. Canon 5 of the American Bar Association's Code of Professional Responsibility, "A lawyer should exercise independent professional judgment on Behalf of a Client," is interpreted by some as prohibiting lawyers from practicing as mediators, but others feel that mediation is an appropriate use of their services. The American Bar Association has, however, approved the practice of mediation by lawyers.

The majority of mediators devote roughly one-third of their professional time to their mediation practice. The remaining time is spent in the practice of another profession such as therapy or psychology. My practice is somewhat unusual as I am a full-time mediator, which means that my only professional practice is that of mediation.

I began my professional career as a therapist in a community mental health clinic. At the time, many separating and divorcing individuals were requesting counseling. In those days, however, the issues of separation and divorce were not considered significant enough to deserve special psychological attention, and the patients were typically diagnosed as suffering from mental disorders. The stages of divorce were not yet recognized by therapists, and individuals were treated for a variety of supposed psychological disturbances.

It became more difficult for me to function within this setting, so I began a private therapy practice, specializing in the problems of separating and divorcing individuals. My interest in divorce prompted me to take law courses and to attend divorce court proceedings. To supplement my income, I began working for the federal Internal Revenue Service, and discovered how the financial and tax aspects of divorce were often ignored.

Shortly after this period, I divorced from a twelve-year marriage and discontinued my therapy practice, as I felt I could not maintain my objectivity in the face of my personal dealings with divorce. My husband and I used divorce mediation to reach our settlement. My interest in mediation increased, and after resuming my therapy practice, I took mediation training and began work for a court program that mediated small claims, assault and battery, and landlord-tenant disputes.

Seven years ago I ended my counseling practice and began a full-time mediation practice. Many of my colleagues felt that this was not a wise move, as I was giving up a successful practice and venturing into an unknown field. But I believed in mediation and felt it offered the only alternative to the trauma of adversarial divorce. My goals for my own mediation practice and my hopes for the growth of divorce mediation have been realized more quickly than I had dared to hope.

Until recently, professionals desiring mediation training had to travel to New York or California to be trained. (In fact, by 1983, almost one-half of all mediators had been trained by Jim Coogler, the "father of mediation.") But mediation training is now available in several states from a variety of sources including nonprofit agencies, professional organizations, and private mediators. (I am the President of Divorce Mediation Associates, which offers training for divorce mediators in New England.)

More than half of all private divorce mediators began their practice as recently as 1981. In most professions, the number of years in practice gives a clear indication of the experience of the professional, but this is not as true for divorce mediators, because the profession itself is a new one. A more accurate indication of a mediator's experience is the number of cases mediated.

Currently, no state offers or requires licenses for mediators. The profession is, in fact, in the early stages of formulating credentials for itself. Several national and local professional mediation organizations have already established standards for their members. These standards usually call for a specified amount of training and supervision and provide guidelines concerning issues such as impartiality, full disclosure, and neutrality. For example, many professional mediation organizations have standards limiting the number of professional roles a mediator may assume with a client. In other words, a mediator who is also a therapist may not offer couples counseling and subsequently function as a mediator with those same clients. A lawyer functioning as a mediator for a divorcing couple may not represent one or both of these clients during any type of legal hearing, nor file divorce papers for them.

It is very likely that some kind of mediator certification procedure will be established within the next decade. This is a rapid timetable compared with the professions of law, psychology, and social work, which established their credentials over centuries rather than decades.

The best way to find a mediator is to get a referral from a friend who has used mediation or from a professional who is knowledgeable about mediation. If, however, you don't know anyone who can refer you, here are some suggestions.

Begin by checking the yellow pages for an association of mediators. If there is no listing, ask a professional who is involved in divorce-related areas, such as a therapist, psychologist, lawyer, divorce center staff member, court clerk, or minister. You may want to attend a divorce workshop or seminar to meet someone speaking on divorce. You can also check newspaper listings for support groups and contact them to see if they make referrals. A college or university may have a course or a center on dispute resolution, and they may be able to suggest a mediator.

After obtaining the name of a mediator, your next step will be to call for preliminary information. Ask if there is any written material that can be sent to you. If you do not want to receive an envelope that says "divorce" on it, be sure to mention that detail, as many mediators have this word as part of their professional logo. If you feel the mediator might be someone you would want to work with, schedule an initial appointment. Since you may want to meet with more than one mediator before deciding whom to hire, explain that you are interviewing and inquire about an introductory session. Ask if this session is free or if there is a charge.

Before hiring the mediator, consider the kind of information you will want to know about this professional. On the telephone or during the initial session, you may want to ask the following questions:

1. What issues do you mediate?
2. What percent of your practice is devoted to mediation?
3. Do you belong to a professional association of mediators? If you do, does this group have required or voluntary standards? If it does, are you committed to these standards?
4. Do you have another professional practice? If so, what is it?
5. What mediation training have you had?
6. How many mediations have you done?
7. What is your experience/knowledge in:
   negotiation or dispute resolution
   therapy
   finances

taxes
pensions
divorce law

8. Will we have confidentiality during our sessions?
9. What is the average number of sessions that we will attend?
10. How much do you charge? Is there a separate charge for services such as telephone calls and the final Memorandum?

There is some disagreement concerning how much substantive knowledge a mediator should have regarding child support guidelines, marital property laws, pensions, alimony statutes, and other divorce-related areas. There are those who believe that a mediator can work within any area of disagreement and does not need expertise in all areas in order to mediate. However, the majority of mediators, myself included, who work in the area of divorce, maintain that a mediator needs this background. I strongly recommend asking a potential mediator about his or her knowledge in divorce-related areas, as I have indicated in question 7.

During the initial session, be alert to these qualities in your mediator:

- A respectful attitude.
- An ability to respond to your questions.
- A substantive knowledge of the areas of divorce.
- A willingness to give each person equal opportunity to take part in the session.
- An unbiased attitude toward you and your spouse.

You should feel that the mediator is competent and trustworthy. Do not hesitate to ask questions, and expect answers that make sense. Remember that you have the right to consult with more than one mediator before hiring someone. Listen to your intuition, then make your decision and begin mediation as soon as is practical.

WHAT ARE MEDIATION GUIDELINES?

Mediation guidelines are rules of conduct that are used during the mediation sessions to create a cooperative environment conducive to reaching agreements. The mediator usually begins the initial sessions with an explanation of the general guidelines. Though these may differ with each mediator, there are more similarities than differences. You will find that most guidelines are based on good sense and common courtesy. To give you an idea of what mediation guidelines are like, let me describe the ones that I use in my practice.

The first important rule is that all sessions remain confidential—neither myself nor my notes may be subpoenaed into court. This agreement is part of the divorce mediation contract that the couple signs with me after the introductory meeting, before the mediation begins (see appendix I). Many believe that this confidentiality is one reason why mediation succeeds in areas where courtroom procedures fail. For instance, courtroom battles involving visitation of minor children in which one parent is an alcohol or drug abuser rarely reach an easy settlement because the individual is often unwilling to admit publicly to abusing alcohol or drugs. The opportunity to reach a private agreement in mediation allows these individuals to create an appropriate parenting schedule. For example, one client agreed to see her children before noon, as she did not drink early in the day. Her husband would have had a difficult time in court proving that she drank, and it is extremely doubtful that she would admit to this activity.

Another important rule in mediation is that clients must disclose all assets, income, and liabilities. My guidelines call for verification of these by having clients bring in copies of their accounts, income statements, and liabilities. Clients in mediation save money by doing the legwork of verification themselves; the adversarial method depends upon a time-consuming and expensive discovery process to verify assets.

Another general rule is that each client may consult with any other professional at any time during the mediation, though I ask that they mention the consultation. It becomes obvious soon enough anyway, as a client's language inevitably reflects the professional advice they have received. I refer clients to other professionals whenever necessary, especially to tax planners, accountants, real estate and business appraisers, as well as therapists and lawyers.

One of my rules may surprise you—the rule that either party is free to change his or her mind in making decisions. Experience has proven that only the freedom to change one's mind results in long-term commitment, which is the chief goal of mediation. Since the majority of clients are hearing information concerning divorce for the first time, they need time to assimilate it and to feel comfortable with their final choices.

Another rule stipulates that neither client has to sign the agreement; they are each free, indeed encouraged, to take the Memorandum and have it reviewed by another professional of their choice. Invariably it stands up to all scrutiny, as it should. A mediated agreement lasts when each person knows that it is a good agreement.

Not surprisingly, physical violence, threats, or coercion of any type are not allowed. Physical violence is rarely a problem in private mediation, where the clients themselves have chosen mediation, but it is a controversial area within court-mandated mediation. I have taken the position as a professional that there can be no mediation while there is the threat or the reality of physical abuse.

Within my practice, I meet with clients individually when necessary. These individual sessions are called caucusing; they may be needed for a variety of reasons, such as extreme levels of anger, the noninvolvement of one party, extreme emotional reactions that make it difficult for both clients to be in the same room, or severe time constraints. Mediators differ concerning this policy; some caucus regularly, others never.

The final mediation rule is that either party may quit at any time. The rationale for this is the same as that for allowing clients to change their minds while making agreements: the freedom to leave results in the ability to make conscientious decisions.

As a mediator, I also have guidelines for myself. Every mediator has a duty to be impartial. This doesn't mean that I do not have feelings or opinions, rather that I do not take sides; I remain neutral. My interventions are based not on siding with one person but on helping the parties to reach fair resolutions.

Mediation works best within an environment that encourages respect. I listen to my clients and they, in turn, listen and respond to each other. I treat my clients as responsible adults capable of making their own decisions, and this usually inspires responsible interactions. I refuse all interruptions from outside sources during sessions to show my respect for my clients' time. People dislike being treated in a manner which says that they, and what they have to say, are not important. You would be surprised by the number of favorable comments I have received over the years regarding uninterrupted sessions. Treating couples with respect sets the stage for them to treat each other with respect.

Guidelines allow the mediator to set the stage for the negotiations that follow. Experience has shown that clients value guidelines, as they help to create a supportive setting within which the difficult issues involved in a divorce settlement may be discussed.

WHY CAN'T YOU MEDIATE YOURSELVES?

Many people have reached a divorce settlement without a courtroom battle or without mediation, but these tend to be cases in which the marriage was short (under seven years), there are no children, and the spouses have comparable incomes and minimal liabilities. If a divorcing couple in this type of situation does try to negotiate their own settlement, their negotiations will be less stressful if they have been separated for at least six months.

It is unrealistic to expect to work out a settlement with someone you are divorcing if any of the following apply to your situation: the duration of your marriage was seven years or more, you have minor children, you own a house or any other real estate, you and your spouse have more than $50,000 in assets, you both have $2,000 or more in liabilities, only one spouse receives a paycheck, you have been separated for less than six months, you have a history of disagreeing or an inability to communicate with each other, or one spouse has significantly more financial knowledge than the other.

There are two main reasons that make it extremely difficult to mediate your own divorce settlement. First, the end of a significant relationship involves emotional turmoil that makes it difficult for two individuals to resolve issues fairly without professional assistance. Second, most individuals do not have the specific knowledge necessary for making informed decisions in divorce-related areas. For example, a couple may think that the pension in the husband's name automatically belongs to him, not realizing that the law in their state considers pensions a marital asset. Or a spouse may attempt to waive rights to an asset without even knowing its value.

I have gotten calls from separating people who tell me, "We've already divided everything up and just want it formalized." More often than not, the list was made by just one spouse, with the other spouse simply going along with the idea. In every case that I have seen, the couple has left out at least one important area, such as future support modifications or real estate responsibilities. Frequently, there are serious omissions that, by law, must be included in a settlement. There aren't any statistics on these types of do-it-yourself settlements, but it is safe to say that uninformed decisions generally do not have good track records.

If you think about it, mediation, with the help of a mediator, really is a do-it-yourself operation—you are the ones making the decisions.

9

Do You Need a Lawyer If You Use Mediation?

"In early Greece, republican Rome, and dynastic China, there were rules against paid legal advice," says Jerold S. Auerbach, in his book *Justice Without Law*. Many separating individuals wish this were true today, fearing that lawyers will sabotage their mediated divorce settlement.

There is little agreement as to whether a lawyer is needed during mediation. Some divorce professionals insist that a client must have a lawyer during mediation, while others forbid all contact with a lawyer. My policy is to neither require nor forbid such contact but to suggest that each party consult with a lawyer at some point during the mediation. Mediation is an open process, and as such, the client should decide whether and when to consult with other professionals.

You do not need a lawyer to get a divorce. Our Constitution allows each person the right to represent himself or herself in court, as long as that person is not mentally disturbed, incompetent, or an infant (which is the legal word for minor).

Some people are reluctant to contact a lawyer for fear

that it will lead to an adversarial contest, which is what mediation clients are trying to avoid. You can minimize this possibility by attending a mediation session before consulting with a lawyer. The important point to remember is that it is lawyer control, not lawyer contact, that is the crucial issue.

Not everyone needs or wants a lawyer during mediation; however, if you do want one, for whatever reason, or if you need one (because of certain complex legal issues), you can use the services of a lawyer and still fully take part in the mediation process.

If you choose to consult with a lawyer during the mediation, you can ask your mediator to provide you with the appropriate questions to ask. Chiefly, what you want to find out is your best deal/worst deal range, that is, what are the best and the worst settlements for property, support, and custody that you might receive in divorce court based on your particular situation. It is at best a guess, as the law is not black-and-white in the area of divorce.

If you decide to use a lawyer during mediation, there are several important questions you will want to ask. (A good time to discuss these concerns is during your initial consultation with the lawyer.)

1. Are you supportive of divorce mediation?
2. Have you ever had a client in mediation? (If the lawyer's answer is no, you need to describe mediation and the fact that you will be the one making the decisions. If the answer is yes, ask about the lawyer's experience.)
3. Will you work with the mediator and support the procedure?
4. Are you comfortable with the fact that I will be the one making the decisions?

5. What is your fee for this type of legal work?
6. What is the most I could receive in a court-contested division of our property?
7. What is the least that I could receive?
8. What do you think is a probable settlement?
9. What is the most child support or alimony that I could receive in a divorce courtroom decision? (Or, what is the most child support or alimony that I would have to pay in a divorce courtroom decision?)
10. What is the least amount of support that I could receive in a contested court trial? (Or, what is the most amount of support that I would have to pay in such a trial?)
11. Who would receive custody of our minor children in a courtroom case?

A lawyer wants to be hired and will almost surely provide those answers that emphasize your best deal. Rarely will you be given responses that will be unpleasant for you to hear and might make you try another lawyer, so it is important to ask the necessary questions and to listen carefully. (Keep in mind that the potential settlement range can be disturbingly broad, through no fault of the lawyer's.)

Typically a divorce lawyer provides only one aspect of your best deal/worst deal range—namely the best deal, the *most* that you (the lawyer's potential client) could possibly receive. The low end of the range is not provided unless you clearly, and sometimes persistently, ask for it. You should be able to elicit the information by specifically asking, "What is the least property division and support that I could possibly get in court?" and "What is the range of the property division and support that I could get in court?"

To give you an idea of why lawyer contact is best held off until after a mediation session, let me describe what happened to clients of mine, Sarah and Larry. Sarah had consulted with a divorce lawyer prior to their first session. During the introductory mediation appointment, she said that her lawyer had advised her that she could get 100 percent of the equity value of the marital residence. I asked her if her lawyer had indicated, or if she had asked, if there was any chance that she wouldn't get 100 percent or that she might get a smaller percentage of it. "No, she didn't mention it," Sarah replied, "and I didn't ask." I suggested that she might want to clarify the answer she had received. At the next mediation session, Sarah repeated what her lawyer had subsequently responded: "Of course, there's a good chance you'll get a lot less. One hundred percent of the house is the best settlement you could possibly receive from the judge." The original 100 percent figure was only a small part of the total amount of information that Sarah needed to be able to make a reasonable decision. Once Sarah had the larger framework of the settlement range, she and Larry were able to reach an agreement.

Consulting with lawyers needn't create difficulties in mediation, though it can be problematic when the more financially knowledgeable party wants to consult a lawyer and the spouse does not. I handle this potential problem by explaining at the introductory meeting my policy, that if one party chooses to consult with a lawyer, both parties should do so.

If you decide to use a lawyer during mediation, you will need to take an active role with him or her. The lawyer will want to push for what he or she perceives as your best deal. However, this may not be in your best interest for a fair divorce settlement. For example, is it in your best interest to have a settlement in which your ex-husband is uninformed and agrees to child support payments that are much higher than the support guidelines in your state? After you pay the legal fees incurred in reaching this settlement, you will most likely end up back in court when your ex-husband realizes that he is not required to provide such high payments and petitions the court for a lower support figure. The support modification might well be lower than he would have originally agreed to because he may be able to show the court that you (through your lawyer) were taking advantage of him. The judge just might show his displeasure with you or your lawyer's actions by ordering low child support. Furthermore, it is not your lawyer who will pay the price; you are the one who will receive lowered payments, and you will also pay the legal fees for this dismal turn of events!

How a professional performs for you is dependent on your control of him or her. This is especially important in your interaction with divorce lawyers. The failure to maintain control is the primary reason for exorbitant legal bills and escalating battles. If you walk into a divorce lawyer's office and say, "Do whatever is necessary to get me a divorce," don't be astounded by the size of your bill. As a client, you need to keep control of the professional who works for you, asking appropriate questions and explaining what you want done or not done. Douglas, a client who came to mediation after retaining a lawyer, failed to control his lawyer and suffered the consequences. His wife, Caroline, had not consulted with a lawyer. At the end of the first session, Douglas told us that his lawyer would be serving Caroline with the complaint for divorce by sending a sheriff. Caroline was furious. Douglas claimed that he did not want this done, but his lawyer had insisted. Douglas maintained that there was nothing that he could do about it. I pointed out to him that he had hired the lawyer and was responsible for his actions. Douglas insisted that he could not change anything, and the mediation ended. Later I heard that Caroline was so angry with Douglas that she hired a lawyer, who obtained a vacate order (a court order to get out of the house), served by a sheriff in a patrol car.

Douglas was clearly not an appropriate candidate for mediation, as he failed to take responsibility for his actions. Clients in mediation cannot escape responsibility by blaming others, whether they be relatives, lawyers, friends, or agents. Douglas failed to realize, or to admit, that hiring a lawyer to do his dirty work didn't mean that he wouldn't pay the price for those actions. If you find it difficult to control your lawyer, remember that mediation can help you retain control.

Many of my clients have had at least one appointment with a divorce lawyer before attending their first mediation session. Sometimes it is this very appointment that has convinced them to try mediation—not as a result of the lawyer's recommendation but because the client is dismayed by the lawyer's adversarial approach. Legal advice may include such draconian measures as a court order forcing the spouse out of the house, emptying joint bank accounts, or changing all the locks on the doors. A client may realize that this kind of behavior will intensify the spouse's anger, create bitterness, and result in prohibitive legal bills. A wise client may realize that these actions should only be taken as last resorts, not as the first course of action.

Sometimes clients who have retained a lawyer before they began mediation question whether they can still use the mediation process. The answer is yes, though the success of the mediation may depend on the client's ability to control the lawyer and on the attitude the client takes toward negotiated settlements.

141

Legal consultation and mediation are not mutually exclusive. Indeed, they can work together quite well if the lawyer is supportive of mediation and if the client is informed and takes control. If you decide to consult a lawyer, your mediator can refer you to one who is supportive of mediation and specializes in the practice of family law. Mediators are often good resources for referral, as they have some expertise in various professional areas and soon learn who performs best.

WHAT IS THE ROLE OF A LAWYER DURING MEDIATION?

During the introductory meeting, I explain to clients the various roles that a lawyer may play in their divorce. If you have any questions about using a lawyer, you should discuss them with your mediator. There is more that your lawyer can do for you than simply being your advocate in court.

During mediation, lawyers may provide ongoing advice in complicated legal situations. This was the case with Ethel and Brad. Ethel was the president of a holding company and had considerable financial knowledge and expertise. Brad, on the other hand, earned a minimal living by writing music, and had no expertise, and even less interest, in finances. Both Ethel and Brad wanted to negotiate their own settlement, and we discussed the various options available to them to reach decisions. The option they chose was to have Brad engage a business lawyer who would be closely involved in the discussions. Their property division negotiations focused on sophisticated financial matters in which they were able to reach a settlement that both felt was fair and reasonable. This case also illustrates one of the most exciting aspects of mediation—its flexibility, which allows it to accommodate virtually any type of arrangement that benefits the participants.

When clients pick up erroneous information (whether from well-meaning friends, TV programs, lawyers, etc.), I sometimes refer them to lawyers to help serve as reality testers. A client with an extremely unrealistic idea of his or her probable legal outcome, or one who refuses to understand the reality of the choices they are making, can be helped by hearing a lawyer's advice. Obviously, the lawyer's attitude toward mediation is crucial; the lawyer should be supportive of mediation, experienced in divorce, and honest.

In the case of Mark and Sharon, a lawyer acting in the reality-testing role was extremely helpful. Mark maintained that if he went to court, he would be awarded the engineering business in which he was the sole stockholder and president. He based this on the court-ordered settlement of his friend, who was a painter and had been awarded his small business. However, the facts of Mark's situation were vastly different. His friend's painting business was a small one-man operation, while Mark's company was a successful firm that employed thirty-five full-time employees. Mark was insistent that any lawyer would get him this "deal," that is, award him the business as his share of the marital assets. I referred Mark to an attorney, and when he heard his best- and worst-deal range, he and Sharon reached a reasonable settlement.

Some mediation clients use lawyers because they have other legal work they want done at the same time as the divorce. They might be transferring real estate or writing new wills, and their state requires the use of lawyers for these documents. In these cases, I provide my clients with a list of appropriate lawyers who handle real estate and wills. Some professionals within the divorce field insist that a lawyer should review the Memorandum before the court filing is done. While I have no objection to this, it can be a rather late time to be getting input from a third party, and can create complications. The spouse may react angrily to the idea of renegotiating the Memorandum and may justifiably resent changes at this late date. If you want this type of legal input, it makes more sense to get it near the start or in the middle of mediation. The potential for harm is minimized if legal advice is received at the beginning of mediation.

After the mediation, a client may choose to have a lawyer file the divorce papers. Some lawyers attach the Memorandum to their document, whereas others write a new document incorporating the Memorandum. Either way is fine, but before hiring a lawyer, be clear about what will be done and how much it will cost you. If one spouse has employed a lawyer to turn the Memorandum into legalese, it may be appropriate for the other spouse to hire a lawyer to review this legal document. In any case, if one party employs a lawyer, the spouse may have to consult with one. The majority of states restrict a lawyer to representing only one party during a divorce action.

In the majority of states you do not need a lawyer to get your divorce. In fact, some states have divorce clinics to help you fill out the various forms that must be filed.

While it is unusual in private mediation to have lawyers present during the mediation sessions, this sometimes occurs in court-imposed mediation. Mediators agree that this is not a good idea except in unusual circumstances, as the lawyers tend to dominate the discussions. The mediator ends up mediating between the lawyers instead of between the clients, as the clients have very little control over their lawyers. Courts that impose this situation and call it mediation tend not to understand what mediation is.

There is a trend in this country toward representing yourself in a divorce action; this is called *pro se*, which means do-it-yourself. Many states now allow this procedure, and it is gaining in popularity both because it reduces the possibility of engaging in a battle with your spouse and because it costs less. Some states now offer summary judgment, where the court staff helps you to file and you may or may not be required to appear in court. Japan has what is called an administrative divorce, and divorcing people in that country do not appear in court unless they are contesting their settlement. This is common in most legal settlements in the U.S. but not in divorce. Normally, Americans do not go to court unless there is a dispute. Divorce is unusual in that the parties must appear in court, even if there is no dispute between them. Perhaps this will change sometime soon.

Men and women in mediation make their own decisions; that is one of the strengths of the process. You may choose to use lawyers, and they may—indeed should—give advice, but you must take responsibility for the actions that result. When you give your decision-making power to someone else, it may feel good for the moment, but in the long run, people who do not take part in their own financial and personal decisions often live to regret it.

10

How Will Using Mediation Help Your Children?

In 1927, the well-known movie star Clara Bow, the famous "It girl," and the new matinee idol Gary Cooper costarred in a melodrama called *Children of Divorce*, which depicted the doomed path of children whose parents divorce. The young boy and girl grow up taking part in illegal and immoral activities, and eventually kill themselves. This Hollywood portrayal of the fate awaiting children of divorced parents reflected the feelings of American audiences over sixty years ago: that if you divorce, you are dooming your children to a life of misery. Some would argue that the present public attitude may not have changed significantly over the years, while others point to the opinion expressed by many of today's experts that divorce is better for children than living in an unhappy household.

One of the reasons that divorcing men and women choose mediation is because of the benefits for their children. There is no question that a divorce settlement agreed to by both parents will benefit the children, even as a courtroom battle is certain to do them great harm. Statistics indicate that the number of children living in single-parent households has increased: one out of every two children under the age of eighteen spends some time in a single-parent family. In any one year during the 1980s, twelve million children lived with a divorced parent. Yet to date there has been little substantive research on the effects of divorce on children. (The scant research available is focused in the area of child support compliance, and these are not encouraging reports. More on this issue in the next chapter.)

One exception to this lack of data is the work performed by two researchers, Judith Wallerstein and Joan Kelly, who in 1971 began a long-term study of the effects of divorce on children. Their research provides information concerning an issue that many people have strong opinions and feelings about but that lacks much scientific evidence.

The Children of Divorce Project was based on sixty families in Marin County, California, a predominantly white, middle-class and upper middle-class group of divorcing men and women with children. The children were interviewed during the divorce, again eighteen months later, and again five years later. Recently the researchers have released the newest data accumulated at the ten-year mark.

The results indicate that "34 percent of the children and adolescents appeared to be doing especially well psychologically . . . while 29 percent were in the middle range of psychological health." The remaining one-third of children described themselves as unhappy, though they did not necessarily have psychological signs of depression or difficulties in school. Significantly, the most important factor in the children's psychological well-being was found to be the attitude of the two parents toward the divorce. Children who are doing well emotionally have parents who are relatively conflict-free in their interactions with each other. Mediation can make this type of interaction a reality by helping to resolve conflict between parents, by defusing anger, and by promoting communication in even the most difficult of marital relationships.

Let's look at an actual case to see how mediation can help children of divorce. The following situation was a difficult one for everyone involved, including the professionals consulted. Elizabeth and Jason, a young couple with a seven-month-old daughter, Stacey, were referred to me by a probate court judge who was apparently frustrated by their repeated returns to court, their habit of ignoring his rulings, and their inability to agree on parenting arrangements.

Jason and Elizabeth had married when Elizabeth found out that she was pregnant. She was barely out of high school and was working as a clerk in a discount store. Jason had been working almost a year in a local warehouse. They moved into the apartment above Elizabeth's parents. Her parents as well as his played key roles in the constant disagreements and arguing that dominated the short-lived relationship. The arguing had escalated after the birth of Stacey. The only thing they agreed on during the initial mediation session was that they should divorce.

The couple had separated four months prior to our first session. They had been to court on five separate occasions because of visitation disagreements over Stacey. Early in the first mediation session, it became clear that Jason and Elizabeth's parents played a central role in their children's relationship. Both sets of parents disapproved of the marriage and apparently fueled the bitterness between the young couple. Elizabeth hated Jason's mother, and Jason seemed to be terrified of Elizabeth's mother.

Prior to mediation, during their last court appearance, the judge had ordered that Jason be allowed to spend a long weekend with Stacey during her six-month birthday.

Jason had been confused over Stacey's formula, not knowing what kind she took nor how much to give her, and his
attempt to ask Elizabeth for information ended with him
swearing at her instead and rushing to his mother's with
the baby. When Jason returned Stacey to Elizabeth, Stacey
had a high fever, and Elizabeth's lawyer had promptly pe-
titioned the court to stop all visiting. In response, Jason
had asked his lawyer to file a court request allowing him
to have Stacey for a two-week visit during the summer. It
was at this point that they were referred to me, when Jason's
lawyer suggested mediation to the judge.

During the first session, Elizabeth and Jason expressed
great anger and lashed out at each other repeatedly. Because of the intensity of their anger and their inability or un-
willingness to refrain from displaying it, I felt the best way
to resolve their conflict was to meet with them separately.

During the individual sessions, each described their reaction to the separation. Elizabeth was upset that Jason had
shown little interest in Stacey's care while they were living
together, and felt that his mother was behind Jason's interest in having Stacey spend time with him now. Jason
explained that after leaving the marital apartment, he began
to want more contact with Stacey, but he was not certain
how to care for the baby and turned to his mother for help.
I saw that they could be helped to work together to care
for Stacey if their parents were removed from the adversarial battlefield. Together they could create concrete
guidelines for Stacey's care.

The problem of their parents' interference was a pressing
issue that stood in the way of their making any successful
arrangements. This was an issue that a judge could not
address but that was essential if this couple were to come
to an agreement. What was needed was a temporary agree-

ment that their parents stay out of the parenting arrangements. During mediation, they decided that none of the grandparents could be present at the time Stacey was picked up or returned, nor could a grandparent pick her up or drop her off. More importantly, they also decided that neither of them would report to the other anything that his or her parent had said, period.

After this temporary agreement, their relationship calmed down somewhat and they were able to make rational decisions about Stacey's care. Jason agreed to a decrease in the hours of visitation with Stacey. He said that he had not even requested such long visits, but that he thought the judge had given him them because he had become irritated with Elizabeth's defiant attitude. In return, Elizabeth agreed to provide information concerning Stacey's caretaking, verbally as well as in writing, and not to undermine Jason's attempts to spend time with Stacey.

This agreement may have been written when Stacey was too young to know what was going on, but she benefited the most from having parents who learned to stop the war and to start negotiating. These young people had seventeen and one-half years of parenting together ahead of them, and they received help before it was too late. The adversarial court system had simply made matters worse by providing them with a battleground. Had Jason's lawyer not suggested mediation, and had this particular judge not recommended it, Elizabeth and Jason would most likely have spent years in court—with Staccy growing up as the courtroom prize in bitter visitation disagreements. Instead, an appropriate referral by the court resulted in significant change for Elizabeth, Jason, and Stacey.

Each child responds to a separation or divorce according to his or her age at the time of the divorce. Even infants such as Stacey have emotional responses to separation and divorce. The child's reactions usually occur in three general stages. The initial feeling is emotional pain: they hurt. Virtually every child whose parents separate, even those who are living in abusive homes, where one might think that the child would experience relief when the abusive parent moves out of the house, experiences some degree of hurt. Keep in mind, however, that painful feelings are not indicative of your having made the wrong choice. The end of any type of relationship—no matter how painful or destructive that relationship was or is—may bring on the feeling of loss.

After this initial pain, the child experiences fear, anger, depression, and guilt. These feelings do not necessarily follow any preordained sequence. Indeed, some children seem to experience all these feelings simultaneously, while others show no emotional reaction, keeping all their feelings from others, and unfortunately, from themselves.

Eighteen months to two years after the separation, the child adjusts to his or her single-parent family. However, children who must cope with many changes at once—such as moving, starting a new school, or combining their family with another—often take longer than this to make the transition to the new family structure. A support group for children whose parents are separating and divorcing, often offered through the school, provides an excellent opportunity for your child to interact with other children who are experiencing a family breakup. This type of shared experience is important for children, who tend not to share their feelings with other children. At any time during this two-year period, perhaps at the time of the separation, perhaps later, your child may need short-term individual counseling, or family counseling with one or both parents and siblings.

Though mediation will not eliminate the emotional hurt caused by separation and divorce, it can reduce it and help parents avoid causing deeper pain. It can also pave the way toward emotional healing and adjustment. The mediation process can help your child by providing these benefits:

- Mediation increases the communication between you and your spouse and allows parents to talk to each other. Increased communication is the first step toward negotiation. The ability of parents to communicate, even if it is limited to one hour a week in a mediator's office, has immeasurable consequences, all of them extremely positive, such as decreasing the anger between the parents and not forcing children to choose sides in the divorce. Any improvement in communication between the parents directly benefits the children.
- Mediation reduces the conflict between you and your spouse. Whether parents are loudly screaming at one another, or silently exchanging bitter stares, your child picks up these messages and is adversely affected. The more intense the disagreement, the more your child suffers. When the parents are helped to resolve a dispute, whether it is the weekend visitation schedule or the division of the employee stock plan, children directly benefit.
- Mediation creates a cooperative attitude between you and your (ex)spouse, sparing your child the difficult role of a go-between. Florence Bienfeld, a leading authority on custody mediation, writes, "When parents are helped to cooperate, their children are more likely to find happiness and satisfaction." This is especially important when a child has a problem: a cooperative attitude allows both

parents to work together in their child's best interests.

- Mediation reduces the time required to negotiate your divorce settlement, whereas the adversarial system is notorious for extending the negotiation period. A mediated settlement typically takes two to three months, while the adversarial approach easily takes one to two years. The time factor is especially important for a child, since a divorce that takes two years to settle becomes the predominant life experience for a six-year-old. Children, even more than adults, need to put the divorce behind them and get on with living their lives.

- Mediation helps you to adopt a flexible role in the parenting schedule of your child. Studies have shown that the majority of parents dislike, and do not abide by, court-imposed visitation schedules. Indeed, many disagreements between parents ensue over inflexible visitation schedules. A schedule that calls for the noncustodial parent to pick up their child at 6:00, when that person doesn't get out of work until 5:45, serves only to fuel the misunderstandings between divorced individuals. A rigid schedule, created by the court in an attempt to reduce conflict between the parents, often contributes to conflict. Mediation helps people to adopt a stable schedule, which has flexibility but is not rigid, and reduces the potential for disputes.

- Mediation allows for future changes as your children grow. Though future changes may seem an obvious requirement in a visitation schedule, court-imposed schedules rarely include provisions for these. A child's needs for parental interaction change over the years, and the successful visitation schedule reflects this. For example, it may make perfectly good sense to pick up little Jennifer at 8:00 A.M. on Saturday morning. At two and one-half years old, she has already been up for two hours! However, at age thirteen, Jennifer does not want to know what a Saturday morning looks like. Yet her parents often do not know that they can create a new schedule, nor do they know how to go about making the change. In mediation, parents learn how to negotiate significant future changes.

- Mediation does not allow your children to be the pawns, or the trophies, in a divorce contest. The mediator's approach is, "What arrangements are best for you, your spouse, and your children?" There is no room for the adversarial stance, "Which of you will win the children?" The belief in mediation is that children offer parents an opportunity to work together, not to compete with each other.

Let's look at another case study of former clients to see how the children, who were never present during the mediation sessions, benefited. My first session with Sharon and Kurt occurred within two weeks of their separation. The family consisted of Kurt, owner of a small appliance store, Sharon, an elementary school teacher, and their eight-year-old twins, Eric and Matt.

During the review of their marital history, Sharon stated that she was leaving Kurt because of his drinking. Kurt did not deny drinking and said that since they were divorcing what he did was his business and Sharon did not have the right to order him about or to insult him.

In a courtroom, it is doubtful that Kurt would be considered an unfit parent: he was not the stereotypical drunk. He held a well-paying job and his drinking did not interfere with his many social and civic activities. In fact, Kurt said that his lawyer had assured him that his drinking would not be a serious issue in court. Sharon's lawyer had advised her that the court would take Kurt's drinking into account if he admitted it (which Kurt made clear he would not do in a public courtroom); otherwise Sharon would have to produce sufficient legal proof.

In mediation, the visitation schedule is determined by both parents based on the best interests of the children as well as the individual interests of each parent. It was agreed that Kurt's drinking would be discussed only insofar as it affected the children. Kurt said that he was just as concerned about the children as Sharon was. He described his drinking and said that if he did have a drink during the week at home, it was around ten at night. He suggested that he could return the children to Sharon's before 9:00 P.M. on weeknights. Sharon thought that this worked well for weekdays but felt that the real problem was weekends, which was when he drank the most, and she did not want him to have the children on the weekends. At this point a verbal battle seemed about to break out, which would not have been productive. Instead, I caucused with each of them individually.

Their final agreement called for Kurt to have weekend contact with his children, but Kurt agreed that he would limit the contact to times when he was not drinking. He felt that it would be best if he did not see the children on Friday or Saturday nights, and he agreed that during the days he had them, he would not take them to events or activities where he was apt to drink.

In all probability, if Kurt did not admit to his use of alcohol in court, a judge would have given him weekend visitation. Mediation, however, gave this family the opportunity to create a schedule that took their particular strengths and weaknesses into account. Both Kurt and Sharon felt that this agreement did not compromise either one of them and that it benefited Eric and Matt.

HOW DOES A MEDIATOR HELP YOU CREATE A PARENTING PLAN THAT IS BEST FOR YOU AND YOUR CHILD?

The most important factor in the well-being of children is the attitude of their parents. Psychologically healthy parents who respect, love, listen, and show their children that they care will have the best chance of rearing well-adjusted children. During mediation, the best interests of your children will receive attention; you are helped to consider their needs as well as your own.

In the adversarial system, courts and lawyers focus on the best interests of their clients, which are invariably the adults in the case, to the exclusion of the children's needs. This is evident in the typical court-ordered visitation schedule, which often orders long periods of time with an infant or a toddler, despite the fact that extended periods away from the primary caretaker may not be suitable for very young children, except in non-traditional situations.

Courts cannot take the time to determine each family member's needs, nor are they trained to help with positive parenting arrangements. Mediators, on the other hand, are well versed in helping people to set up workable visitation patterns, or will refer clients to appropriate therapists.

You can use a mediator to help you with a parenting plan at these times:

1. Before a physical separation, to help you to decide how much contact children will have with each parent, and under what conditions.

2. During the separation, to help resolve a dispute between the parents, or between one parent and a child, or to create a new schedule.
3. After the divorce, for the same reasons listed under number 2, only now these are legal schedules that have been ordered by the court.

Many parents come to mediation for help in making a parenting schedule. Few parents know exactly the kind of visitation arrangement that will work for them. Often parents need basic information and help in setting up a working plan; sometimes they are in conflict and want help in resolving the dispute; and occasionally they simply want to check out if what they are doing is beneficial for their children.

Divorce mediation began with custody disputes. Donald Soposnek, a noted child custody mediator, described these disputes as "the mediator stepping lightly over a minefield." Though mediators cannot resolve every custody dispute that ends up in their office, they offer the only hope of resolving these disputes with satisfactory results. Court decrees that award a child to one parent without the agreement and support of the other parent create anger and resentment that lead to future custody disputes, visitation arguments, and kidnapping. The benefit of a mediated custody dispute is that both parents have had a say in the final settlement.

Though mediation began with custody disputes, most of the cases that I see concerning children are in the area of visitation. Let me provide a short example of how a mediator can help with a chronic visitation problem.

Marie and Larry had been to court on thirteen separate occasions over their son, Chris. Marie was the primary parent for Chris, and Marie and Larry constantly argued over each other's parenting of Chris. Chris, by the way, was seventeen years old.

The disputes this year occurred regarding Chris's needing a ride home when his work shift ended. Chris called his mother for a ride home; Marie would then call Larry to provide Chris with a ride, and they would argue if Larry said no. It was apparent that the fighting between Larry and Marie was an old pattern, and new rules needed to be created if there was to be a positive change. The plan I helped them create was to have Larry responsible for bringing Chris home on specific nights. We arrived at a schedule that both parents created, and we agreed that Marie would not call Larry about the rides. Each parent, by the way, was fearful that the other would not live up to his or her end of the deal. They knew each other well— the first week, each of them twice failed to carry out the agreement. The second week, only Marie called Larry once about a ride, and by the third week, neither of them had reverted to their old, enmeshed pattern.

Parents who decide on joint physical custody also may run into problems. Paul and Nancy decided on joint custody and set up a plan that provided for each to have their two young daughters for roughly equal amounts of time. The parents were well-meaning, and they were confused over the behavior of their young children. Though divorced, they continued much of their marital interaction; for example, they prepared and ate dinner together every night of the week. Neither parent could understand why every meal ended with their two young children hysterically screaming for Daddy not to leave. Carol Whataker, a well-known family therapist, writes that "Children whose parents got divorced stop wishing them back together when the kids are about eighty-one years old." I helped Paul and Nancy work on creating interactions that would be helpful and clear to the children, in light of the new structure of two separate families, rather than continue a pattern that was upsetting to everyone, despite the best of intentions.

A mediator can help create a visitation schedule that meets the needs of all family members, though some members, specifically the children, may not actually be in the room. In unusual cases, the children are brought into the mediation sessions. Again, one of the strengths of this procedure is its flexibility. Couples who have worked out all the financial issues of their divorce may still turn to mediation to help with the visitation issues. A mediator's assistance and guidance can make a profound difference to a child. Take the case of Doreen and Greg and their youngest child, fifteen-year-old Ricky, who were helped enormously by professional intervention.

Doreen and Greg had been married for twenty-two years and had four children. At the time of the separation, the oldest three were out of the marital house and living on their own. Greg and Doreen lived in an old house that was constantly in need of repair, and Greg was buying the house from Doreen. She was relieved to move out of the house, and had asked Ricky where he wanted to live. Ricky, in a choice typical of adolescents, told his parents that he wanted to remain in his school and neighborhood, so he chose to stay in the marital residence.

Ricky was very angry at Doreen for moving out, and Doreen felt that it should be up to him whether or not he would see her. By the time I met with this family, Ricky had not seen his mother since the separation six months earlier. Greg complained that since Doreen had left, Ricky just wanted to argue with him all the time. Both parents noted that his last two report cards showed that Ricky was not doing very well in school.

Two months before their introductory mediation meeting, Ricky had been injured while playing hockey. His coach had driven him to the hospital, and a staff person had asked him for his phone number and address. He had given the phone number and address of his mother. Doreen rushed to the hospital to be with him, but after his release, she was afraid that their contact would revert to the old pattern. Sure enough, Ricky did not call her, and she did not call him.

During their second session, we discussed Ricky's need for contact with both his parents, and I explained the adult responsibility to initiate contact. By the end of the session, they set up a weekly time for Doreen and Ricky to get together. By the last session, Doreen said that she was seeing Ricky, and though he expressed some anger, he had shown up every week. Greg commented that Ricky was not fighting with him nearly as much as he had been.

Although divorce is difficult on children, living in a troubled household is also difficult, and may be more of a problem. There is enough information to suggest that divorce may actually help a child by removing him or her from a negative situation.

One year after the mediation has ended, I call my former clients to find out how the provisions of the agreements are turning out. One client relayed this account to me: "My son Brian was turning eight at the time of his father's and my separation. As you know, our friends thought we were a compatible couple since we rarely argued in front of people and put up a good front. But I was under a lot of stress, and I was very unhappy during the last two years of my marriage. After my husband moved out, I watched for signs of problems with my son because of the separation. Within a month, I was surprised when a neighbor told me, 'Brian has been whistling every morning now when he comes by to get Josh for school.' I guess I hadn't realized that separation could also lessen the tension that he had been living with."

A mediated custody and visitation settlement makes a significant emotional and practical difference in the life of your child. By helping parents to communicate and to focus on the best interest of the child within an informed and cooperative setting, mediation reduces the emotional impact of divorce on those who perhaps suffer the most, yet have the least say in the process—your children. Mediation helps to give children a voice.

11

How Will Mediation Affect Your Future?

One of the primary reasons that divorcing individuals choose mediation is because of the positive impact it will have on their future. Several studies, as well as my own observation, attest to the concrete ways in which mediation promotes a better postdivorce adjustment than the adversarial approach. Here are some of them:

- You will feel that the divorce settlement is fair. I am occasionally asked if one person can win everything in mediation. The answer is no. A good mediator intervenes to balance the power and helps the couple to work out a fair settlement—not just any kind of a settlement. The attitude of fairness is an important one to have in an agreement that you will live with for many years!
- You will not be paying off high legal bills. This future benefit may not seem important at the time of the divorce, as most bills come in after the divorce is final. It is difficult to start a productive new life with high fi-

nancial debt. In many adversarial domestic conflicts, $60,000 to $70,000 is not an unusual amount to pay for a divorce. While it may not be unusual, few of us can afford to spend that amount of money. Since a divorce results in two household costs instead of one, there is a need for each spouse to minimize expenditures and conserve assets so that there will be enough to divide between the spouses.

- You are unlikely to return to court on a divorce-related issue. Approximately one-half of all divorced people who have used the adversarial approach return to court after their divorce. This is not true for mediated divorces. Judge Dorothy Beasly, of the Georgia Court of Appeals in Atlanta, stated, "If two people each contribute to reaching a final solution, they'll own the decision, and they'll follow and respect that decision much more than one handed down by a judge."

- You and your ex-spouse will have a more civil relationship with each other. Many divorcing men and women start off with good intentions—they don't want to join the ranks of those couples who have had bitterly contested divorces—but the adversarial divorce process has a way of escalating anger between two people. Most couples experience a lot of anger toward each other when they separate. If this anger is encouraged, as in the adversarial system, the relationship deteriorates rapidly. If the anger is defused, as in mediation, the anger lessens and the relationship will improve naturally as time goes by.

- You will have the ability to negotiate future issues. A common question from clients is, "What if we need to change our divorce agreement?" One of the strengths of mediation agreements is that change is part of the format. The Memorandum may call for the two of you to negotiate between yourselves, or, in more difficult areas, to use a mediator.

- You will most likely pay less in federal taxes. When two individuals are able to cooperate, the total tax bite can often be reduced. In contrast, individuals who use the adversarial approach may end up contributing the maximum amount to Uncle Sam. It usually takes working together to minimize tax liabilities.

- If you are an alimony recipient, you are more likely to receive your payments. Statistics vary; the American Bar Association reports that within two years of a divorce, over one-half of all alimony recipients were not receiving their support or were receiving severely reduced payments, while a study by Professor Lenore Weitzman of Stanford, California, showed that one out of every six individuals were not receiving alimony. Many ex-spouses who are forced by the courts to pay alimony will try to get out of it. (The new child support compliance provisions that are being introduced by federal, state, and local governments to collect support payments are not available for alimony recipients.) The men and women who choose to pay alimony in mediation have agreed to do so of their own free will, and are more likely to continue to do so.

If you are a parent, mediation will have a profound effect on your children's future as well as on your own:

- Your child will be better adjusted than if you and your spouse had used the adversarial approach. Research on the emotional effect of divorce on children has barely begun, but we do know that reduced animosity between parents is reflected in the better emotional adjustment of their children.

- Your family will have a more workable and harmonious custody and parenting schedule than a family in which the court was forced to order custody or visitation. Courts often mandate "reasonable" visitation but do not define the term, and parents continually disagree over what is reasonable. When parents make custody decisions together, their children have the best arrangements, regardless of the specific plan.

- The custodial parent is more likely to receive child support payments. Nationwide, only one-third of parents who are awarded child support through the adversarial approach actually receive the full amount. A quarter of the parents who are entitled to child support do not receive one penny. Millions if not billions of dollars in child support go unpaid.

  Contrary to popular stereotypes, nonpayment of support obligations is not linked to any one income level. Studies have shown that middle-income and upper middle-income parents are just as likely to avoid paying child support as are low-income parents. The use of mediation to address child support matters creates a dramatic increase in child support compliance.

- You will most likely have made provisions for the payment of your child's undergraduate expenses. As recently as ten years ago, divorce settlements did not typically address college expenses. Today, however, mediated agreements usually include a provision that provides for the payment of college expenses.

The most well-known mediation study is the Denver Mediation Project. It was carried out by Pearson and Thoennes at the Center for Policy Research in Denver, Colorado, and sponsored in part by the Colorado Bar Association. In March of 1979 mediation services were offered to Denver couples who were divorcing. The couples who used mediation, as well as those who did not use it, were studied and evaluated. According to the study, the mediation couples:

- Expressed greater satisfaction with the final divorce agreement.
- Were optimistic about resolving future property issues with their ex-spouse.
- Felt the property division was fair.
- Had better compliance with the provisions of the settlement.
- Had not returned to court for postdivorce court action.
- Reported better understanding and communication with their ex-spouse.

Those mediation clients with children also reported that they had a higher number of joint custody agreements and enjoyed more contact with their children than did couples who did not use mediation.

You may be interested to learn what the future held for some divorcing men and women who used the adversarial approach. The following case summaries are, unfortunately, not only true but typical.

Two years after her divorce was final, Marsha began dating. She invited her new friend, Todd, to dinner to meet her two children. Two days later, Marsha's ex-husband called and told her that he did not want her new boyfriend to see the children again. He hung up before Marsha was able to utter a word.

Three weeks later, Marsha took the children to play miniature golf with Todd. One week later she was served with a summons to appear in court for a change in the custody award because of the legal neglect of her two children. Marsha was extremely upset by the allegations, though she knew they were completely untrue. Their first hearing was continued—in other words, postponed—to a later date. (She never did understand the legal reasons for this.) On her way out of the courtroom, her ex-husband bluntly told her that he was going to keep forcing her to appear in court if she dated other men.

Marsha went back to court several times on this case, but finally the judge dismissed the charges against her and continued her custody award of her minor children. Marsha's legal expenses amounted to $5,200, she missed eight days of work, and all she can do is wait and wonder if her ex-husband is going to drum up other charges to force her back into court.

Donna and Ray are another example of the hazards of the adversarial method. They had been married for eighteen years prior to their separation, a separation they both wanted. Both were employed in financially secure occupations, though Ray made $100 a week more than Donna. After deciding to separate, they consulted briefly with lawyers but basically worked out a financial settlement on their own.

Briefly, the agreement called for their total savings accounts and stocks, a little over $30,000, to be equally divided between them. Donna was to receive the condo and one-third of Ray's pension, as she did not have a company pension plan. Both agreed that there was to be no alimony. They would each take responsibility for their respective car loans and divide the approximately $3,000 in charge card debt. In addition, and this was an important point to Donna, Ray would cosign the loan for Donna's educational expenses (she had recently applied to an MBA program).

Shortly after this, they retained lawyers. Donna's lawyer, after being paid her retainer and after several appointments, told Donna that she should ask for alimony. Donna did not feel that she should receive alimony, but her lawyer explained that it was simply a negotiating strategy.

Over two years and $33,000 later, Donna and Ray were standing in front of a divorce court judge. All negotiations between the lawyers had broken down, and Donna and Ray were no longer on speaking terms. The judge finally granted a divorce. The settlement stipulated that Donna receive the condo and, instead of the pension, ordered Ray to pay her $20 per week. The savings and stock were gone, used up to pay legal expenses on both sides. Ray had long since refused to cosign for the educational loan and Donna was not able to afford school.

Donna is bitter over her divorce process. She and Ray had a reasonable settlement that both felt was fair, and Donna says that she is most angry at herself for listening to her lawyer, though she is pretty mad at her lawyer, too. Donna is considering returning to court with a new lawyer, if Ray refuses to go to mediation, for he has never paid the $20 per week that was ordered, but Donna knows that her legal expenses would cost more than the money owed, and anyway, the last she heard, Ray was no longer employed at his old job.

Mediation would have made a big difference for Donna and Ray, and it will have a significant impact on your future. If the two of you own only a knapsack and the clothes on your back, mediation can still make a difference by reducing the anger and expense associated with the adversarial approach. If you have been married for a long time, and have some assets, mediation will make a greater difference. And for those of you who have children, mediation will have a beneficial effect on your child's future adjustment.

12

Divorce Mediation: The New Alternative to Adversarial Divorce

The U.S. has one of the highest divorce rates in the world. During the 1980s the rate has leveled off at a little over 50 percent, which means that there is one divorce for every two marriages that take place today. United Nations demographers predict that the U.S. rate will climb to two out of every three marriages by the turn of the century. However, the cost of an adversarial divorce has not leveled off and continues to escalate dramatically. Very few Americans remain untouched by divorce.

Divorce is an emotional and physical crisis second only to the death of a loved one. No matter how many men and women divorce, it is a personally devastating event. Yet in spite of the personal, legal, and financial difficulties facing divorcing men and women, society offers them virtually no support. We do not mourn divorce in the same public manner as death—sharing sadness with wakes and funerals—nor do we celebrate the end of bad marriages. Instead, divorce courts are filled with anxious people, accompanied, if at all, by paid advocates. Divorce is ultimately experienced alone: "Laugh and the world laughs with you, cry and you cry alone."

Along with the emotional pain and the monetary expenses of divorce, divorcing people must deal with court procedures that are frequently regarded as insensitive. To begin with, court systems in many jurisdictions are so backlogged that a wait of one to two years is not uncommon. A practicing divorce lawyer describes the system as "riddled with hypocrisy and perjury." Stanley Rosenblatt, a divorce lawyer in Los Angeles, California, wrote in his book *The Divorce Racket*, "There are millions of silent Americans who know that divorce in this country is a tragic farce." Divorce laws are in chaos; court workers know it, lawyers know it, judges know it—and divorced individuals know it best of all. Divorced men and women invariably walk out of a divorce courtroom feeling bruised and resentful. It feels as if the divorce process is your punishment for choosing to divorce.

In so many ways our country leads the world, but not in our archaic divorce system. In law, procedure, custom, and attitude, other countries are more progressive, humane, and efficient. In Japan, a country that has a divorce rate one-third of ours, and in Sweden, which has a divorce rate one-half of ours, divorce is obtained in an administrative process set in motion by the mutual agreement of the spouses. These countries reserve judges and courts for criminal activities and unresolved conflicts.

Every day of the week, 3,200 men and women in the U.S. get divorced. It is an astonishing figure. Perhaps it is the magnitude of these numbers that is contributing to changing attitudes toward the divorced and reforms intended to help them. There are now no-fault laws in all fifty states; support groups, seminars, and workshops on divorce issues; clinics and agencies offering assistance; changes in the IRS code on capital gains in marital transfers; federal and local statutes enforcing child support compliance; and supportive therapists who treat divorce as an emotional crisis and not as a sign of mental instability. These changes underline the growing desire by many divorcing individuals and the professionals who work with them to find more rational and less abusive ways to deal with the end of marriage.

Mediation is the only serious alternative to the adversarial approach since that fateful day in 1661 when the General Court in Plymouth, Massachusetts, granted the first divorce in the New World. Now men and women are attempting to recapture some of the decision-making powers that our courts wield.

On January 1, 1981, California became the first state in the nation to mandate that all contested custody and visitation disputes use the mediation process. One year later, Jay Folberg, chairman of the American Bar Association of the Family Law Section, in his lecture at the San Francisco Plaza Hotel on May 20, 1982, predicted that within ten years mandatory mediation laws would be adopted nationwide. His prediction is well on the way to being fulfilled.

Some people wonder how mediation has gained such widespread acceptance within such a short period of time. Only seven years ago, I was speaking in front of a small group on the new subject of divorce mediation. More than half the audience seemed surprisingly relaxed, and I was rather perplexed. Having spoken frequently on various topics of divorce, I knew that most listeners were quite anxious at the beginning of the evening. Indeed, my preliminary comments were always prepared with the goal of reducing the anxiety level of the audience. With the present group, however, I skipped my introductory remarks, reasoning that if they were any more relaxed, they would fall asleep.

Shortly into my talk, I saw looks of surprise and confusion

come across many faces. I stopped and inquired about the confusion. One woman, accompanied by vigorous nods from many in the audience, responded, "I came because I thought it was a demonstration on meditation and I needed to unwind."

Today, people are less apt to confuse mediation with meditation. However, many people are still not sure what mediation is or if it will work for them. I hope that this book has explained what divorce mediation is about. Some critics insist that mediation is not for everyone. It may not be—there is undoubtedly very little in this world that is perfect for everyone. However, mediation is appropriate for the vast majority of divorcing couples. Mediation allows men and women to change their lives in a civilized way that does not punish them or deprive them of their dignity. The reality is that most of you have nothing to lose by using mediation—and a lot to gain.

There are many events in our life over which we have no control, just as there are many events over which we do have control. Whether or not to divorce may feel like a choice to some of you; to others it may not. After the decision to divorce is made, you will have more decisions to make. You have three ways to achieve your settlement agreements: on your own, using lawyers, or using mediation. Hopefully this book has helped you to become aware of the benefits mediation has to offer. Mediation helps you to reach fair separation and divorce agreements in a rational manner that allows you to maintain your dignity. You deserve at least that much and more. You deserve the right to get on with your life.

APPENDIX I

Mediation Contract

We are requesting services from Divorce Mediation Alternative in order to settle issues within our marital state that will allow us to seek separation or divorce agreements under the following conditions:

1. This mediation is voluntary. Either of us may choose to end it at any time.
2. Each of us understands that the mediator is not an attorney and is not representing either or both of us.
3. We will disclose all of our financial worth and assets during the mediation sessions. We may each use professionals as advisers, but each of us accepts full responsibility for the reasonable accuracy of these figures.
4. We will not subpoena the mediator or her files in any court proceeding.
5. The mediator cannot impose any decision upon us.

6. Everything that is said during a mediation session is confidential and will not be used by either person in any pending or subsequent litigation.
7. Either of us may seek professional and legal advice at any time during the mediation.
8. At the conclusion of the sessions, the mediator will prepare a written Memorandum of Understanding, setting forth our agreements. We will each receive a copy.
9. Each of has been advised by the mediator to have separate, independent counsel to review the Memorandum of Understanding before signing it.
10. The mediator will not disclose any information concerning us to a third party without our prior consent.

Mediation Fees:

1. Mediation services are based on a per hour fee of $90.00. Payment is due at the time of each session unless advance arrangements have been made. You may set up a payment plan.

2. Other fees may be charged in addition to the mediation session. These fees are charged at the same hourly rate as above:

   a. Consultation with other professionals.
   b. Document review and interpretation.
   c. Telephone conversations in excess of ten minutes.
   d. Travel time and expenses.
   e. Preliminary and temporary agreements.

3. Preparation of the written Memorandum of Understanding is $245.00. You will each receive a copy of this document at the last session.

Appendix I

I have read and understand the conditions of this mediation contract.

_____   _____

(Wife)   (Date)

_____   _____

(Husband)   (Date)

_____   _____

(Mediator)   (Date)

APPENDIX II

MEMORANDUM OF UNDERSTANDING for Ellen Robertson and David Robertson*

This memorandum was drafted on June 17, 1988, between Ellen Robertson, born Ellen Whitney on December 12, 1948, and David Robertson, born on October 4, 1947.

Background

They were married on June 14, 1969, in Hartford, Connecticut. This is a first marriage for both of them. They moved to Massachusetts in 1972 and lived in the Commonwealth until their separation on January 8, 1988. There are two children born of the marriage: Jennifer, born on February 26, 1973; Jeff, born on January 8, 1977.

The Present Situation

Ellen and their two children are currently residing in the marital house at 00 Main Street, Boston, Massachusetts. David is residing at 000 Huntington Street, Boston, Massachusetts. David has been paying all of the household expenses at 00

---

*Names, dates, and certain details have been changed.

Main Street and providing Ellen and the children with $250 per week.

Divorce
They will file for a no-fault, uncontested divorce.

Present Income
David has been employed as a regional manager at the Metropolitan Company for the past eleven years. His gross annual salary is fifty-one thousand dollars ($51,000). He does not receive bonus or overtime pay.

Ellen has a part-time position at the Boston Public Library for twelve hours per week. She earns four dollars ($4.00) per hour for a gross annual earning of one thousand and nine hundred dollars ($1,900).

Divorce Mediation

David and Ellen reached the following agreements after careful consideration and discussion in divorce mediation:

CHILD CUSTODY

Legal Custody
The parents have agreed to shared legal custody of Jennifer and Jeff. Ellen and David will consult with each other on all major decisions concerning their children, such as education, elective medical choices, religious upbringing, and their general welfare, including counseling decisions. Each parent agrees to keep the other reasonably informed of Jennifer's and Jeff's significant academic, physical, emotional, and social activities and will forward to the other parent copies of all such verbal and written medical and educational communications.

Any emergency problems will be promptly handled by the parent who is present or first reached. The other parent will be notified as soon as possible.

David and Ellen are both committed to their role as parents and they will continue to support each other in their parenting.

Physical Custody

Living Arrangements
The children will live primarily with Ellen and she will make all of the day-to-day decisions.

Parenting Arrangements
David and Ellen want a flexible and consistent parenting schedule and have agreed upon the following guidelines:

Weekdays. David may spend a minimum one evening per week with each of the children, to be negotiated with the child, and David will provide at least one week's notice of the date. He may see them separately or together. He will pick up and return the child to Ellen's residence. He will return Jeff by 9:00 P.M. on a school night until he is fifteen years old.

Weekends. David will spend every other weekend with Jeff. He will pick him up from Ellen's on Saturday morning and return him to Ellen's residence on Sunday between 4:00 and 5:00 P.M.

Vacation. Each parent may spend up to four weeks with one or both children during the summer school vacation. David may spend one fall, winter, or spring one-week school vacation with one or both children. The parents will provide each other with a minimum of one month's notice for any vacation time they want with the children.

Holidays. They will spend these holidays with their children:
David will be with the children Christmas evening (which begins after 5:00 P.M.), every other Thanksgiving (Ellen to be with the children this 1988 Thanksgiving holiday) and every Father's Day. Ellen will be with the children Christmas Day until 5:00 P.M., every other Thanksgiving, and Mother's Day. They will negotiate other holidays as the time approaches.

Travel. Ellen and David will provide each other with reasonable notice prior to taking Jeff or Jennifer outside of Massachusetts or on any trip exceeding three days. If the time with the child involves an absence from school, a parent must obtain prior approval from the other parent, such approval to not be unreasonably withheld.

Religious upbringing. Neither parent will change the religious upbringing of Jennifer and Jeff.

Geographical change of residence. David and Ellen will renegotiate the parenting agreements if either parent moves out of the State.

CHILD SUPPORT

David will provide child support payments to Ellen. Child support agreements:

1. Payments will begin with David's first paycheck after their court filing date and he will pay her every week thereafter within three days of receiving his paycheck.

2. Payments will be 25 percent of David's weekly gross salary, which is currently two hundred and fifty dollars ($250) per week.
3. "Emancipation" is defined as a child experiencing the earliest of the following:
   a. Eighteen years of age and not attending high school nor enrolled as a full-time undergraduate student at a recognized college.
   b. Twenty-two years of age.
4. Child support will end upon both children experiencing the earliest of the following:
   a. Emancipation.
   b. Marriage.
   c. Permanent residence away from the home of Ellen, not including residing at college.
   d. Entry into military service.
   e. Death.
5. There will be a 15 percent decrease in child support payments upon Jennifer's emancipation.
6. Child support will be renegotiated upon:
   a. One or more children living with David.
   b. Ellen's gross income, minus support payments, exceeds $25,000.

MEDICAL INSURANCE AND EXPENSES

David is providing all family members with Blue Cross/Blue Shield health insurance through his place of employment.

Medical agreements for children
1. David will continue to provide this plan or a comparable plan for each child until that child is emancipated.
2. Ellen is responsible for all reasonable uninsured and deductible medical costs for the children, such as prescriptions and office visits.

3. Ellen and David are equally responsible for the cost of any necessary extraordinary medical expenses not covered by insurance, such as therapy or cosmetic surgery.
4. Ellen and David are equally responsible for medical expenses for the children that exceed $500 in any one year.

Medical agreements for Ellen and David

1. David will continue to carry Ellen on his health policy or a comparable medical insurance policy for as long as she is eligible, or he may elect to pay for her insurance premiums through another comparable policy.
2. They are each responsible for their own uninsured and deductible medical costs.
3. If Ellen has reasonable health insurance available to her, she will notify David as soon as possible, and she will provide for her own insurance.
4. If Ellen remarries, she will be responsible for her own health insurance.
5. If David remarries, he will continue to be responsible for Ellen's health insurance premiums.

DENTAL INSURANCE AND EXPENSES

Dental agreements for children

David has a Delta Dental Plan through his place of employment.

1. He will continue to carry the children on this policy as long as they are eligible and as long as he has dental insurance available to him at a reasonable cost through his place of employment.
2. David and Ellen are equally responsible for all dental costs for their children, including orthodontic expenses.

Dental agreements for Ellen and David

1. He will carry Ellen on his dental policy as long as she is eligible and as long as he has the insurance available to him at a reasonable cost.
2. If Ellen or David remarries, Ellen will be responsible for her own dental insurance.
3. David and Ellen are each responsible for their own uninsured and deductible dental expenses.

LIFE INSURANCE

David has the following life insurance policies:

1. A group term life insurance policy through work for one hundred and four thousand dollars ($104,000). Ellen is the beneficiary.
   a. He will continue to carry at least this amount of life insurance as long as he is required to pay child support or alimony.
   b. The amount of insurance he is required to carry may be prorated according to the number of children who need to be supported, but not less than $52,000.
   c. Ellen will continue to be the beneficiary of this amount of life insurance or she will have access to the income.
2. A whole life policy which is David's. He may change the named beneficiary at any time.

SPOUSAL SUPPORT

David will pay Ellen one hundred and forty dollars ($140) per week in spousal support beginning with David's first paycheck after their court filing date.

Spousal support guidelines
1. This support is alimony.
2. Alimony is a fixed amount with an annual cost-of-living adjustment according to the federal Consumer Price Index for the Boston area.
3. Adjustments to alimony:
   a. There will be an adjustment to alimony if Ellen earns over $25,000 per year (not including support payments). The reduction will be one-third of the amount over $25,000 up to a maximum of $35,000.
4. Alimony will end upon the earliest of the following:
   a. Ellen's death.
   b. Ellen's remarriage.
   c. Ellen earns $35,000 or more in one year, not including child support or alimony payments, in 1988 dollars.
   d. David's retirement, not earlier than his reaching age sixty-two.

THE MARITAL RESIDENCE

Their house is located at 00 Main Street, Boston, Massachusetts. It is owned by Ellen and David as tenants by the entirety. There is one mortgage on this property with the Bank of Boston. The balance was thirty three thousand and two hundred dollars ($33,200) as of June 1, 1988.

Use of the marital residence
Ellen will have the exclusive use of the marital house until the earliest of the following:

1. One year after Jeff is out of high school.
2. Ellen moves out of the house.
3. Ellen remarries.
4. Both agree to sell or one person buy out the other's share.

5. Ellen dies, in which case David may move into the house.
6. Neither child is living in the house.

Ellen will be responsible for the following expenses while she is living in the marital residence: real estate tax, mortgage interest and principal, house insurance, utilities and fuel costs.

Rental of marital residence
Ellen may rent part of the house as long as she is living in the house. The rent money is hers.

HOUSE MAINTENANCE, REPAIRS, AND IMPROVEMENTS

House maintenance
Ellen will be responsible for all routine maintenance to their house, such as interior painting, wallpaper, and lawn service.

House repairs
Ellen will be responsible for all repairs to the house costing less than three hundred dollars ($300) per project. They will equally share the cost of any one repair project costing over $300, including exterior painting.

House improvements
They will share in the cost of any necessary house improvements.

Ellen will be responsible for any cosmetic or unnecessary improvement to the marital residence. She will be able to subtract the cost of such improvement at the time of the property sale. She will not be able to subtract the appreciation from such improvement at the time of the sale. She must obtain the approval of David for any project that may result in a lowered value of their residence.

Equity loan

1. Ellen agrees to sign a line of credit or second mortgage to enable David to obtain a portion of his equity in the house. She will sign for him to take up to 70 percent of his portion of the equity in the house.
2. David will be responsible for the equity loan payments and will hold Ellen harmless from any liability connected with this loan.
3. The balance of this loan will not be subtracted from the proceeds of their marital residence at the time of division.

Sale of the marital residence

David and Ellen will sell the house to a third party or one of them will buy the other out of the house (see "Use").

Sale to a third party

They will choose a realtor and set a sales price. Upon the sale of the house, the net proceeds shall be equally divided between Ellen and David. The net proceeds shall be defined as the sales price less:

1. Balance of their first mortgage.
2. Closing costs.
3. Attorney fees for the sale of the house.
4. Realtor's commission (if actually paid).
5. Any amounts both agree to.

Marital residence buy-out

1. If either party chooses to buy out the other's equity, they will each choose an appraiser and average the two prices. If the appraisals are out of line with each other, they will

choose two more appraisers and average just these two appraisals. They will equally divide the net proceeds.

2. The net proceeds shall be defined as the sale price less all of the above except realtor's commission.
3. Ellen will receive the cost of any improvement that was paid for by her.
4. Neither party will cause any lien to be put upon the house. If a lien is placed upon the property, the person responsible for causing it will be responsible for the debt.

HOUSE CONTENTS

David will take the following items from the house with him by the date of their absolute divorce:

Family room set	Linens
Two tables	Green quilt
Two lamps	Books
Some kitchen utensils	Crystal set
Stereo equipment	Cordial set
CD player	Wok
Street scene pictures	Toaster-oven
His records	Magazine rack
Work tools	Living room bookcase
Bike	Sports equipment
His desk	Personal belongings

He will leave the dining room set in the house for at least one more year. All of the remaining items belong to Ellen, including appliances.

VEHICLES

David will keep the 1986 Honda Accord. This car is registered in Ellen's name. They will change the registration to

David's name by the date of their court appearance for their divorce.

Ellen will keep the 1987 Plymouth Reliant. This car is registered in both names. They will change the registration to Ellen's name by the date of their court appearance for their divorce.

STOCK

432 shares of Metropolitan stock. The stock will be equally divided between Ellen and David by the date of their divorce.

PENSIONS

David has a contributory pension plan through his employer. He is vested in this plan. If he continues at his present salary until retiring at age sixty-five, the monthly benefit will be two thousand, two hundred and eighty-eight dollars ($2,288).

Ellen will receive 25 percent of these benefits. She will arrange to have a qualified domestic relations order on her portion of the pension.

They will each keep their respective IRAs.

INDIVIDUAL AND JOINT ACCOUNTS

They will divide the joint Bank of Boston account by the date of the court appearance for their divorce: Ellen will receive $2,300 and David will receive $2,700.

Ellen will keep these funds:

1. The money in her individual checking account at U.S. Trust.
2. Four hundred dollars ($400) in bonds.

David will keep these funds:

1. The balance of the joint checking account with Bank of Boston with which they are paying bills.
2. A Prudential whole life insurance policy with a cash surrender value of four hundred and thirty-five dollars ($435).

CHILDREN'S EDUCATIONAL EXPENSES

1. The parents expect their children to help with college expenses by applying for available scholarships, grants, and loans.
2. The parents will pay college tuition, books, application, school, and laboratory fees for each of their children according to the proportion of their respective average incomes at the time each child attends college. They will average their income and assets for the past four years in determining the amount available for college.
3. Each child has a savings account with under one thousand dollars in it. This money may be used to provide undergraduate education for a child or for another use agreed to by both parents. Ellen will control these funds while the children are under age twenty-two.
4. $600 in bonds will be used toward the children's undergraduate education.

LIABILITIES

Ellen is responsible for the following liabilities:

1. House expenses
2. Her charge cards

David is responsible for the following liabilities:

1. Support payments
2. His charge cards

TAXES

1. They will file their 1988 taxes jointly if they can do so and if it is to each person's financial advantage. They will negotiate a division of any refund.
2. Child support payments are not deductible to David on his federal and state tax returns, nor are they taxable to Ellen on her federal and state tax returns.
3. Alimony payments are deductible to David on his federal and state tax returns and taxable to Ellen on her federal and state tax returns.
4. Ellen has Jeff as a tax exemption, as long as he is living with her.
5. David has Jennifer as a tax exemption, as long as he is current in his child support payments.
6. Ellen will be entitled to any federal tax deductions on their marital residence.
7. Each party is responsible for their respective capital gains tax on the sale of the house.
8. They agree to cooperate on any tax audits or investigations of prior year tax returns.

LEGAL AND COURT COSTS

Each is responsible for their own legal and court costs associated with their divorce.

MEDIATION

David and Ellen have mediated these agreements in good faith. Each has fully disclosed their individual and joint financial holdings and income.

Ellen and David understand that I am not an attorney and that at no time did either of them receive any legal advice from me. Each has been advised to seek independent legal counsel to review this Memorandum and to incorporate the goals reflected here into a legal document.

If there are any further areas of dispute concerning their divorce, they will use the mediation process as a first step toward resolving their dispute.

APPENDIX III

Parenting Schedules

If you and your spouse are unable to come up with a schedule, if you are in conflict, or if you simply want some help creating a good arrangement for visitation, these suggestions may help. These guidelines are suitable for those families choosing a traditional visitation schedule with primary physical custody vested in one parent.

Infants (birth to six months)

- Frequent but fairly short visits.
- Preferably no overnights.
- If visits occur only once a week, they should probably be no longer than one to three hours.
- Physical caretaking—such as scheduling of naps, type and amount of formula, time of feeding, etc.—should be consistent.

Babies (six months to eighteen months)

- If there has been little prior contact with the visiting parent, the visits should initially be short (one to three hours) and frequent.

- If contact has been frequent (daily or every other day), then visits with the child may be extended to longer periods of time.
- Continue to maintain the baby's caretaking routine.
- If possible, visit in the same location every time.
- Overnights may or may not yet be appropriate, depending on the quality and amount of contact between parent and baby, and the practical realities of distance and time available to the parent.
- The visiting parent should try not to leave the child with a caregiver who is unfamiliar to the child.

Toddlers (eighteen months to three years old)

- Overnights are appropriate at this age if the child has been spending time with the visiting parent.
- Weekends may still be too long a period of time to spend away from the primary parent on a regular basis. (Compare this suggestion with the policies of most courts that call for visitation every other weekend, regardless of the child's age. Summer visits, often ordered by the courts for blocks of two weeks or longer, are not appropriate at this young age; three-to-four-day visits are preferable.)
- Maintain usual bedtime hour and eating routines.
- Continue naps if at all possible.
- Coordinate toilet training methods with the other parent.
- Be sure to take along your child's favorite toy, blanket, or other attachment.

Preschoolers (three to five years old)

- Predictability is very important to a preschooler and should be kept in mind when planning the visitation schedule.

- Overnights are within the ability of most children and two-night weekends may be fine.
- One-week blocks of time in the summer and during school vacations are fine for most children.
- If visits are more than one week, it is advisable to have some physical contact between the child and the primary parent.
- It is still advisable to coordinate toilet training habits and to continue bedtime and nap schedules.
- The preschooler can tolerate more variety in terms of foods and discipline techniques.
- Adults can be clear in providing simple explanations to the children. Sadly, many adults feel that children of this age just can't understand and do not provide any explanations. Children need them; indeed, they are entitled to them.

Early Childhood (six to ten years old)

- Visits need to be predictable and specific for the child. Not only should the parents be able to plan their future time, your child should be able to predict where he or she will be most of the time.
- If possible, spontaneous contact is a good idea, so your child feels that you spend more time than is called for. However, it must be coordinated with the other parent in advance. Phone calls and letters between visits are also a useful way to keep in touch, and to show that you are interested in them between visits.
- Overnights during the school week may be fine for most children, as long as a reasonable bedtime hour is maintained.
- Visits every other weekend may be appropriate, though it

is a good idea to keep some contact with the child during the week.

- Most children are mature enough at this age to be apart from the custodial parent for extended periods of time during the summer, though again, the child may benefit from some contact with the custodial parent during any extended visits.

Late Childhood (eleven to twelve years old)

- During the preadolescent years, children often want input into their visitation schedule. They may want their own social activities to play a significant role in the scheduling of their time. Parents may want to consider their child's wishes.
- You may occasionally want to include a friend of your child's during a visit.
- At this age, it is not uncommon for the child to want a reduction in visiting time, yet it is difficult for the visiting parent not to see this as rejection. Keep in mind that the number of hours children are available to their parents is generally starting to decrease, as peers play a more significant role in your child's life.

Adolescence (thirteen to seventeen years old)

- If couples separate while their child is in adolescence, parents may assume that contact with the child could simply be left up to the child, but I do not recommend this. It is up to you to initiate contact, even if you are frequently "rejected." Try not to take rejection personally; remember that it is your teenager's job to become independent of you.
- Your child may not welcome weekend visits, but do not

give up entirely on overnights, and try to accommodate his or her wishes along with some type of one-night visit.
- Time must be arranged with your teenager's busy schedule in mind, yet a predictable and consistent pattern, with flexibility based on your child's activities as well as your own, is still preferable.

Young Adults (eighteen to twenty-two years)

- Young adults do not suddenly lose their need for contact with their parents, but the need is of a different sort. Once again, it is still important that the parent initiate contact, but a young adult is now capable of assuming some of the responsibility for contact.
- During these years, it is not necessarily the amount of time spent together that is important, but the quality of the time together.

INDEX

Abuse
  and child's response to divorce,
    151
  mental, 81
  physical, 23, 33, 50–51, 81, 82,
    93
  sexual, 93
Accidents, incidence of, 49, 88
Accountants, 132
Administrative divorce, 145, 171
Adultery. *See also* Affairs
  as grounds for divorce, 81, 82
Adversarial system, 1–3, 6, 17,
    19, 20, 28, 31, 44–45, 47–48,
    79, 81–82, 136–37, 141, 146,
    166–68, 170–72
  children and, 146, 154, 156
  costs and. *See* Legal costs
  definition of, 4
  emotional stages of divorce and,
    108–10
  emotional stress from, 1, 17, 18,
    20, 38–39, 48, 88, 92, 117,
    122, 171
  fault grounds in, 21–23, 81–82

mediation before or after, 23
time needed for divorce with,
  25, 47–48
Affairs, 26, 50–51
Alaska, 89
Alcohol abuse, 81, 131, 154–55
Alimony, 5, 13, 64, 66–68, 167–68
  compliance with, 164
  postdivorce litigation over, 37
  postdivorce mediation over,
    112–13
  questioning lawyer on, 138
  sample mediated agreement on,
    185
  taxes and, 13, 46, 67
American Bar Association, 126,
  164, 172
  Code of Professional Responsi-
    bility of, 126
American Bar Journal, 25
Anger, 54
  in children of divorcing parents,
    151
  as emotional stage of divorce,
    102–4, 109

Index